"*Weathering Change* brims with wisdom and encouragement for navigating life's many and often-challenging transitions. Drawing attentively and insightfully from God's two books of revelation—the Bible and creation—Courtney Ellis offers practical grounding for finding our footing and even thriving in these turbulent times."

Ben Lowe, executive director of A Rocha USA and author of *Doing Good Without Giving Up*

"Courtney Ellis's *Weathering Change* teems with a tumble of life: Sage Thrashers and ocean tides, falcons and microbes, bears and goldfinches. Amid this kaleidoscopic tour of the earth's wonders, Ellis reveals a shimmering thread of wisdom about managing change. At a moment in history when change feels overwhelming and pervasive, Ellis's witty and gentle prose brings nature's wisdom to bear on our human experience, drawing from her own family life and pastoral ministry as well. Spend a little time with this congenial companion, reveling in delight and wonder and God's provision, and you will feel more at ease with change—and less alone."

Debra Rienstra, author of *Refugia Faith: Seeking Hidden Shelters, Ordinary Wonders, and the Healing of the Earth*

"*Weathering Change* is a wonder and a deep comfort for all who know how change can weather us. Courtney Ellis's refreshingly unusual writing seamlessly weaves readings of creation, Scripture, and some of her own candidly told story into the profound mystery of living in God's world with all its glory and its groaning. Her wise curiosity and her love of nature in general and birds in particular are what make this book about the challenges that change brings to us all so beautifully original. I trust it will find and bless a wide audience of both believers and questioners."

Peter Harris, cofounder and president emeritus of A Rocha International

"Transitions are a tough and awkward constant in life. How we handle transitions builds resilience for those to come. Through hilarious personal stories, practical advice, and descriptions of the natural world, Courtney Ellis opens our eyes to see God has not left us to our own devices. In his graciousness, he has revealed ways through his marvelous creation for us to navigate this world and all it throws at us. Not only did I learn much about birds and bears and even ice in *Weathering Change*, but I finished the book fortified to take on change myself as an opportunity to grow."

Shemaiah Gonzalez, author of *Undaunted Joy*

"There are plenty of self-help books out there about change that offer trite, one-size-fits-all answers. This is not one of them. Courtney Ellis takes what feels like a novel and deeply refreshing approach—to let the wisdom of the natural world guide us through the ebb and flow of change. She approaches the topic not with soundbites and cookie-cutter answers but with reverence, nuance, vulnerability, pastoral wisdom, and more than a dash of humor. This book is a gift!"

Kyle Meyaard-Schaap, author of *Following Jesus in a Warming World*

"Change is hard for most of us. But Courtney Ellis invites us to look with curiosity and wonder at patterns in the natural world and God's unending promises to remind us that, whatever changes come our way, we can adapt and maybe even find delight."

Josina Guess, associate editor of *Sojourners* magazine and contributor to *Bigger Than Bravery*

"As a nature lover, I found it refreshing and encouraging to read Courtney Ellis's exposition of the myriad ways God's dealings with us are reflected in how he has ordered his creation. Caterpillars, birds, changing seasons, migrations, prairies, and wind—all become metaphors for God's work in our lives. A beautiful and inspiring read."

Fernando Ortega, recording artist, bird photographer, and author

"How do we make sense of a world in which change and decay and even despair seem to be all around us? *Weathering Change* is a theodicy, but a strangely hopeful one, a clever metaphysic masquerading as an everyday devotional. Ellis seamlessly alternates between simple daily living and the sublimity of nature in a manner that recalls Terry Tempest Williams."

Ted Floyd, editor of *Birding* magazine and the author of *National Geographic Field Guide to the Birds*

Weathering Change

SEEKING
PEACE AMID
LIFE'S
TOUGH
TRANSITIONS

COURTNEY ELLIS

Foreword by
LORE FERGUSON
WILBERT

ĩvp

An imprint of InterVarsity Press
Downers Grove, Illinois

InterVarsity Press
P.O. Box 1400 | Downers Grove, IL 60515-1426
ivpress.com | email@ivpress.com

InterVarsity Press® is the publishing division of InterVarsity Christian Fellowship/USA®. For more information, visit intervarsity.org.

All Scripture quotations, unless otherwise indicated, are taken from The Holy Bible, New International Version®, NIV®. Copyright © 1973, 1978, 1984, 2011 by Biblica, Inc.™ Used by permission of Zondervan. All rights reserved worldwide. www.zondervan.com. The "NIV" and "New International Version" are trademarks registered in the United States Patent and Trademark Office by Biblica, Inc.™

While any stories in this book are true, some names and identifying information may have been changed to protect the privacy of individuals.

Published in association with the literary agency of WordServe Literary Group Ltd., www.wordserveliterary.com.

The publisher cannot verify the accuracy or functionality of website URLs used in this book beyond the date of publication.

Cover design: Faceout Studio, Spencer Fuller
Interior design: Jeanna Wiggins
Images: © CSA Images via Getty Images, © ZU_09 / DigitalVision Vectors via Getty Images, © Sergey Ryumin / Moment via Getty Images, © bauhaus1000 / DigitalVision Vectors via Getty Images, © Medesulda / DigitalVision Vectors via Getty Images

ISBN 978-1-5140-1282-6 (print) | ISBN 978-1-5140-1283-3 (digital)

Printed in the United States of America ♾

Library of Congress Cataloging-in-Publication Data
A catalog record for this book is available from the Library of Congress.

31 30 29 28 27 26 | 13 12 11 10 9 8 7 6 5 4 3 2 1

TO ALL THE GOOD FOLKS AT

Presbyterian Church of the Master

Contents

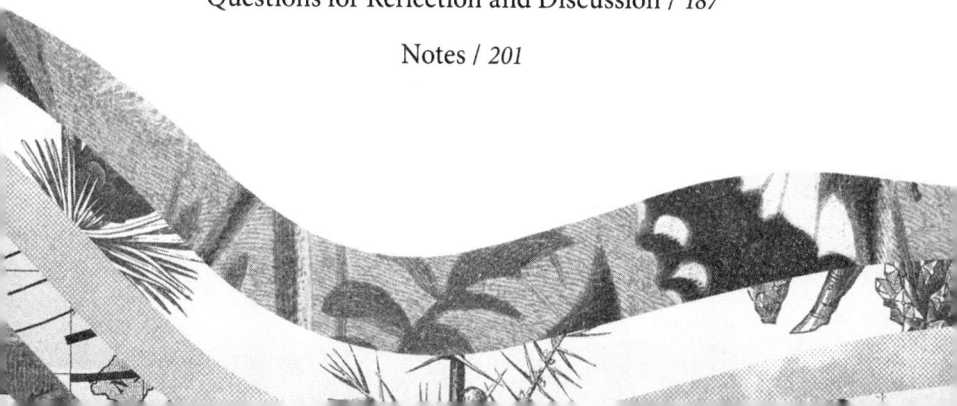

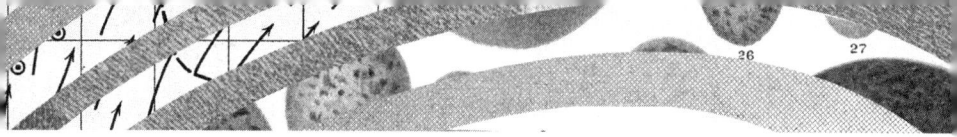

Foreword

LORE FERGUSON WILBERT

DEAR READER,

Whenever I am unsure of what to do, whenever I feel lost or adrift, afraid of the unknown, I resist the urge to look within myself or even take it directly to God in the form of prayer. Instead, I look outside.

The seasons, the scenery, the flora and fauna—all of it teaches me something about life, death, change, birth, loss, renewal, regeneration, and more. The clouds teach me that sometimes the light is hidden, but not gone. The wind teaches me that we cannot always see the work while it is being done. The snow teaches me that deep beneath it is not death, but life, just waiting for the right conditions. Even a still, quiet summer day is showing me the many layers of what stillness will do in me if I let it happen. The lessons are endless and always revealing more and more about who we are and who God is with us.

In this beautiful book, Courtney Ellis brings us along with her on a journey through weather, the seasons, the land, and the inhabitants of this earth we call home. She weaves together her own stories and the stories of birds, plants, water, wind, and soil to show us where to look when everything sure begins to feel uncertain. Courtney does not shrink from death in the natural world, nor gloss over it; she brings a magnifying glass to it, showing us how slow, painful, and achingly beautiful change is.

Books like these are catnip for me. The juxtaposition of story and science, the natural world and spiritual growth—I will never tire of works like these. Courtney has written a book that encapsulates all of this beautifully, and I cannot commend this work more to you.

I hope you bring this book along with you on a hike, or a kayak through still waters, or on a picnic with a friend, or that you read it beside a window with your favorite hot beverage. I hope you take breaks while you read it to—as Courtney taught us in her last book— look up and see what the earth, and the God who made her, have always known: Change is beautiful and necessary and deeply, deeply *good*.

1

Tough Transitions

*It's sometimes hard to tell whether you are being killed
or saved by the hands that turn your life upside down.*

BARBARA BROWN TAYLOR

NEAR THE SOUTHERN PEAKS of the Sierra Mountains lies a cave
that traverses miles underground, worn through metamorphosed
limestone. Lined with stalagmites, its ceilings are home to eastern pip-
istrelle and northern myotis bats. Deep inside, dazzling and macabre
creatures exist fully in darkness—translucent centipedes, pseudoscor-
pions, spiders without eyes.

We drove hours to witness this phenomenon, up the winding highway
into Sequoia National Park, and over a narrow, pothole-studded road.
Crystal Cave is only open to visitors on official park tours, so we'd
booked a noon departure time. Three dozen others stood with us, listening to the ranger's warnings—rockslides, rattlers, poison oak.

When she gave the okay, our kids shot down the trail as if released
from a slingshot. My husband, Daryl, bearded and flannelled, followed.
I struggled to keep up for a quarter mile, limping but determined, until
we rounded a switchback and I could see an even steeper descent ahead.

"Go on," I waved to Daryl and the kids. They hesitated. "I'm not
going to make it," I said. "I'll catch you on the way back."

A week before our vacation I'd dropped a metal water bottle on my
bare toes. The doctor confirmed that nothing was broken, just a severe
contusion, my foot all blues and purples.

"It'll be very painful for weeks," he said. "Only do what you can tolerate."

"Hiking?" I asked, hopeful. He grimaced, handing me a walking cast. We'd planned our entire vacation around exploring California's sequoia forests and coastal redwood trails. We'd waited all year. But here I was, a quarter of a mile in, my toes pulsing with pain.

I would see none of the wonder we'd sought. Instead, I would wait for the group to return while I parked myself on a rock and elevated my foot next to a very ironic park sign: *Weathering*, it read. *Though this outcropping of marble may seem as durable as Sierra granite, it is slowly wearing away.*

"Same," I sighed.

Change is *hard*, whether it's unexpected change, unwanted change, or even positive change. It rocks my world, and I am a person who vastly prefers a rock-less one. I know I'm not alone in this. I'm willing to bet that you can point to particular changes in your own life that haven't felt enjoyable or welcome: an illness or injury, the end of a relationship, a job transition, or even simply aging—that cruel reality that comes for us all. Change is hard. Yet it is also constant.

As a pastor, I spend a good deal of time walking with people through changes in their lives. They come to speak with me after learning that the cancer has returned. They're struggling because the nest is empty, the teenager is wandering from the faith, or the house needs to be downsized. They want to know what to do because they've sensed that their spouse shouldn't be driving anymore or their aging mother might need to move in. How might they cope in the face of these transitions?

Even joyful changes tend to come with a side of grief—a wedding, a new job, a new baby, each can upend nearly everything for a season, leaving us breathless. People sit in my office and pound the table or pull Kleenex after Kleenex from a box. I visit them in their homes or hospital rooms where they do the same. Nothing rattles us quite like change.

So what are we to do? How might we make sense of all the changes we face, both as individuals and as larger groups—congregations, neighborhoods, communities? Is there a way to find hope in a God who promises never to change, even when all around us is shifting sand? This book is a study in what it might it look like to weather change well, to find peace, even amid life's tough transitions. It is an effort to make sense of the ambiguity surrounding change that dwells within our own souls. As Margaret Renkl writes in *The Comfort of Crows:*

> I am not ready to move past the past, but I am ready for something different, too, something new and urgent and thrumming with the blood and sap of life. I am learning that it is possible to want two contrary things at once. I want nothing to change. I want everything to change.

Therein lies the rub.

In his book *Master of Change,* author Brad Stulberg encourages those faced with change—which is to say, everyone—to accept its inevitability as a part of life. When we can learn to embrace change, adjusting to it becomes far easier. "If we can let go of our stubbornness and defiance, then change actually promotes health, longevity, and growth," he writes. This is a tall task, yet it is also one that God invites. The Christian journey is one of transformation and sanctification, after all. As we follow Jesus we become more like him and also grow up more fully into the people God created us to be.

This open-handed adventure can be filled with grace and peace. According to Henri Nouwen, "The compassion Jesus offers challenges us to give up our fearful clinging and to enter with him into God's fearless life." Much of our struggle surrounding change lies in our inability to accept that it is an inescapable—and often even *good*—part of existence. I get it; it's tempting to resist. But change is unavoidable. We can fight the tide all we want, yet our intransigence won't stop it from rolling in.

Time for some good news: God does not leave us rudderless in how we might navigate the winds that rise and blow. We have the guide of the Spirit, of course, and the unique, authoritative, essential witness of

Scripture. Both are invaluable for our walk through this life. But there is a third mentor given to us as well. One that has much to teach. It is God's good creation, the Book of Nature: seminal, beautiful, brutal. God infuses the natural world with guidance in how we might weather change well. And creation isn't simply an illustration as to how we might understand the transitions we face—it holds deep wisdom for our understanding of God, ourselves, and the world. Jesus often points to birds and fields and trees, not as a cheap way to make a point, but because the created order itself testifies to who God is and how we have been created to live.

Nature demonstrates how to prepare for impending change. When transitions arrive, both flora and fauna show curiosity, adaptability, and resilience. When faced with disorder, animals innovate. Plants flex. Insects find a way. And they do this without the anxiety that so often plagues us, their human cousins. When a tiny sea turtle breaks through the shell of its egg on a remote beach, it wastes no worry before slowly shuffling toward the dark and mighty ocean. Nature simply *is*. "The animals are more ancient than us," writes John O'Donohue. "Somehow they already inhabit the eternal."

My favorite teachers of all the natural world are the birds. They speak, not only in songs and calls but in their behaviors, patterns, and presence. They point us heavenward but also toward the rest of creation, its trees and bees, its fish and reptiles and mammals, its mountains and rivers and vast, sandy deserts. Together they paint a picture of a universe studded with God's intention and attention, its wisdom deeper than our bones.

This book will go beyond just birds though. (My last book, *Looking Up*, was all birds all the time, except for the parts that were about death. Though a few sections were somehow about birds *and* death? It's complicated.) It is not that I've grown tired of them—I am convinced that I will never tire of the birds. It is that paying attention to the birds has begun to teach me also about other facets of creation—seasons, for example, and trees. It became impossible to love a Western Flycatcher without also becoming curious about what it ate—not just flies, but mosquitoes and midges and moths too. But what kind of moths? That drew me down the rabbit hole of entomology, which led to lizards, which led to amphibians, which . . . well, you get the idea.

Isn't it just like God to leave the natural world so studded with delights that we discover more with every tree we climb? And not just one or two—a meager abundance—but exponentially more? Our God is not stingy. There are about 11,000 species of birds in the world and 30,000 types of fish. These numbers are estimates because *we keep finding more.* I want to walk through this life with my eyes attuned, don't you? No sunsets are saved for later. Every pilgrim walks a path marked by beauty, adorned with hope.

In this book, I will bear witness to some of the ways plants and animals make their homes in the in-between times and places, on the edges and margins, amidst the many transitions they face. It's a book written out of my own need: I want to learn how to weave a nest for my tender young amid the perilous spikes of a succulent like a Cactus Wren or discover how to turn a blackened forest into a foraging ground like a Canada Lynx. I need to believe that if Blue Whales can grow bigger than school buses by eating only tiny krill, then I can look for the flashing silver of nourishment just below the storm-tossed surface of things too.

I don't wonder whether creation has lessons for us in our struggles with change—I *know* that it does. The Book of Nature boasts a deep well of wisdom indeed, if only we might be faithful to study it. Waking up to creation is a life-long journey and joy. I love how ornithologist and poet J. Drew Lanham puts it: "Nature asks only that we notice."

Here I'm seeking deeper and fuller answers to two questions I suspect are nearly universal. The first is this: Why is change so damn hard? The second is its deeper companion: How might we find peace amid life's tough transitions? I suspect that the answers to both will not come in prepackaged words. The lessons written throughout the Book of Nature don't show up as simple formulas: *Do X and weathering change will be easier.* Creation tends to favor more subtle instruction. Its wisdom shows up in experience and mist and metaphor, the sprawling parables of Jesus to a waiting crowd who just wanted to be told what to do.

"Do you still believe in God?" a student asked my birding friend Paul, a former Baptist pastor who now teaches physics and astronomy.

"Let me show you my duck photos," answered Paul.

For years I have read and observed and studied in an effort to shape a theology of change. As I did, I noticed four distinct qualities of how creation weathers it: *preparation, curiosity, adaptability,* and *resilience.* The rest of this book is arranged according to these categories. We will delve deeply into what the natural world models for us in each one and the ways we can begin to understand the echoes of ourselves that are written into each element of creation. In doing so, we may begin to find ourselves home at last in a world that is constantly shifting under our feet, even as it continues to move beneath us.

It won't be easy—change never is. Learning to weather change will inevitably change us as well. But if God can send Abraham out to look at the stars and minister to Elijah with ravens and answer Job out of a raging whirlwind, I have no doubt the Spirit is speaking to each of us through the natural world too. Let us tune our eyes and ears and hearts to the voice.

Above all, this book is a twofold invitation. First, it is my version of the women at the tomb saying, "Come and see." Together we will investigate how the natural world responds to and copes with change. But to do so, we must first and regularly engage in the spiritual practice of noticing. Of becoming aware of the world God is building around us with all its wild magic. Of tuning into bizarre realities like miracles and holiness and resurrection, wingbeats and fungi and breezes and soil.

Second, the invitation is this: The next time you are facing change and feeling unmoored, distraught, confused, frustrated, terrified, or just plain out-of-sorts, go outside, take a deep breath, and look around. Then, tell of your own wonders.

Preparation:

readying yourself for what is coming or may come.

Preparation ensures that we are better equipped to deal with impending change. For example, as winter approaches, pear-shaped Willow Ptarmigan molt out of their red and brown summer feathers into pure white plumage. Then, when winter arrives, their new color helps camouflage them against the snows of Alaska, Canada, and Siberia.

Preparation can help us feel more at peace with change, knowing that we have done what we can in advance to ease the transition.

2

Stasis

The invisible world can speak to us.

TERRY TEMPEST WILLIAMS

MY HUSBAND, DARYL, AND OUR KIDS and I have one little apple tree in our front yard, a gift left behind from our home's previous owners. It stands eight feet tall, its gray branches supple but strong, its leaves the greenest green, bright like limes. We still have much to learn about horticulture, but we dutifully prune it back once a year according to the instructions of a local orchard. The tree ends up looking so forlorn, a sheared sheep. I'm always afraid we've cut away too much. But then the other 364 days of the year we leave it alone, adding just a little water or fertilizer here or there. After it winters—a season of rest and recovery, a time of stasis, of preparation—it blossoms again in summer, producing its fruit in the early autumn. The pruning is essential and even a little bit brutal, but it is not what happens to the tree most often.

Before there is change, there is order. Often brief or fleeting, but possible. For a time, life remains stable, certain, balanced. This is stasis, our baseline. We are at rest. These seasons are essential to human flourishing, for it is then that we can grow, enjoy the fruit of our labors, and live at peace. During times of calm we can prepare for whatever is next. It's what creation does.

Stasis comes from an ancient Greek word that means "standing," and indeed, times of stability are where we find our footing. We can't run or even walk until we have a stable place upon which to stand.

Every branch that does bear fruit he prunes, Jesus tells his disciples, but nowhere does he tell us that we are to be constantly stripped bare. There is pruning and then there will be time for healing—and growth.

Nature depends upon seasons of peace where things are left undisturbed, unshaken. So do we.

The first church I pastored sat on the edge of a highway in a town called Clinton, a farming outpost in Wisconsin's Rock County. Smack in the middle of Wisconsin's southern border, just north of the great state of Illinois, Clinton was a place of equilibrium. Many of the families—I'd even dare to say *most*—had been there for generations. A unique patience, a long-suffering of sorts, settles in when a community of people have been bearing with one another for decades upon decades, weathering collective and individual tragedies, celebrating milestones, slogging through long winters. There are feuds, of course, and grudges long nursed, but all is Cold War, not hot. I suppose that if you know you'll see that neighbor you dislike six days a week for the next sixty years, it's best to find your way toward at least a stalemate.

The seasons came and went with regularity—winter, planting, growth, harvest. Clinton was a farm town, first and foremost. Corn grown for animal feed and sprawling green fields of soybeans. Noisy pig farms and, a few miles down the road, rich, ripe-smelling dairies. The landscape featured squatty brown hay bales and silver silos that popped up on plowed fields like agricultural spaceships. We had a forge and a farming company, our own K–12 school and seven different churches, all for just over two thousand people. Clinton's Main Street felt positively Norman Rockwell-esque, filled with tradesmen and women: a hairstylist, a postmaster, a florist, a mortician. After spending my educational years amid the hustle of Chicago, Princeton, and Nashville, the town of Clinton felt like a welcome back into simpler times. It was Americana of the 1950s, diners, striped barber pole, and all.

When Daryl and I flew up from our home in Nashville so I could interview for First Presbyterian's pastorate in early October of 2010, the hiring committee pulled out all the stops. We were welcomed with a potluck dinner and hayride, pumpkin carving, fresh-picked apples, and a toasty bonfire. When Daryl began to shiver as darkness fell, one of the men disappeared into his house and came back with his own flannel barn jacket to hand over.

After a decade of feeling sized up by whoever was in a room—the intelligentsia, the political, the wealthy—the charism of Clinton blew through my soul like a cool breeze on a scalding day. I felt freed to be myself again: the self that grew up in the forests of northern Wisconsin, who wore hiking boots to church and cut her own hair, who chose clothes based on coziness and function rather than trend. I felt seen once again for my heart and not the airs I could put on or the handbag I carried, coming back down to earth after years of walking a tightrope. I knew how to be *me* here.

I hoped this could be home. I could think of no better place to learn how to be a pastor.

People of faith have described seasons of stability as essential for centuries. Augustine described the peace of an ideal city as having a tranquility of order. Terese of Liseaux encouraged remembering that continual striving and change were not necessary, teaching that holiness consisted simply in doing God's will. Richard Rohr's wisdom pattern notes that disorder and reorder can't come unless there is first a season of order—*stasis.*

These church mothers and fathers have also long acknowledged that stability is not a time to retreat into sloth, complacency, or distraction. Stasis must never be confused with stagnation or staleness. It's an opportunity. A window that may be quite brief. We can let it pass us by or we can make the most of it. After all, the time to shore up a ship is long before the storms arrive. Because if life teaches us anything at all, it is that storms *will* arrive. Stasis is an essential gift of time when we may rest, recover, celebrate, and also lean into deeper work.

Yet it is one of life's conundrums that the simplest of instructions can also be the most difficult. Stillness? *How?* Like sharks, we want to keep swimming, lest we die. In the stillnesses, we fear that all we've been staving off—anxiety, worry, anger, the realization that we really should get that mole checked out—will come rushing at us like a train. Busyness is a protectorate, a shield against all we are loath to face. As Paul Kingsnorth puts it in *Savage Gods,* "Stillness is the really hard work." Plus, if we are still, we might even hear from the Almighty. And what will become of us then?

Yet it is in the silence and stillness that we might find ourselves again, freed from the pressures to *go* and *do.* God has created us for rhythms of work and rest, activity and stillness, transition and stasis. Nature is constantly changing, always in flux, yet it is sometimes also very, very still. The wind blows where it will, but it also dies down from time to time, leaving a rippleless lake, glassy waters reflecting every leaf in the trees that line its shores.

We will struggle to weather change if we cannot also weather stillness. Each day will have enough trouble of its own.

Our church's preschool raises Monarch caterpillars. The pudgy zebra-and-yellow-striped insects live on potted milkweed plants encased in butterfly nets erected to gently protect them from curious children. In the late spring these caterpillars, filled to bursting with milkweed leaves, spin bright green chrysalises around themselves, intricate homes that are both delicate and sturdy.

I always imagined that caterpillars basically just hibernated while growing wings, never looking closely enough to see that an adult butterfly resembles a caterpillar about as closely as you or I do a toaster oven. While the adult insect is slender—black thorax and spindly antennae, delicate legs and curled mouthparts, paper-thin wings covered in colored, chalk-like scales of orange and white and black—the juvenile is a thick, striped tube designed for chomping leaves into energy. Its stubby, hooked feet cling to branches. Its mouthparts never stop crunching, crunching, crunching. A butterfly looks nothing like an adult caterpillar should.

If we look a little closer, we will discover that a caterpillar doesn't simply turn black and thin out, growing wings out of its back like a Pegasus. No, inside that chrysalis, it dissolves into goo. If you snipped open the caterpillar's home midway through its metamorphosis, you would not find a half-caterpillar, half-butterfly. You would find a sticky, unformed mess that looked nothing like either and would quickly wither and die in the light of day. But this brownish sludge, when protected by the strong chrysalis, is nurtured in darkness. At the proper time, a butterfly will emerge. God only knows how. Scientists are still figuring it out, though they have discovered that it involves breathing tubes that somehow don't dissolve when almost everything else does and magical structures called, I kid you not, *imaginal discs*, which are hormonally activated within the chrysalis to turn into the butterfly's body parts. Nature is so metal.

The butterfly reminds us that stasis is not the same as nothingness; it is a time of rest, but it is also often a time of preparation. The hearty breakfast we eat before the cacophony of the day begins will sustain us through the morning. The Scriptures we sow into our hearts in peaceful seasons will remain with us when upheavals arrive. Stasis is an opportunity to quietly ready ourselves for what comes next: we lift the weights, save for the tuition, write the will. A chrysalis is silent and still, a jeweled sleeping bag hung precariously on a twig, but inside the wonder of metamorphosis goes on.

As Aslan tells Lucy Pevensie, "There is a deeper magic at work." There nearly always is.

A few of our preschoolers, witnessing one butterfly's final moments of trial as it worked to emerge from its confines, wanted to help it along. The impulse is a kind one—watching a creature struggle can tug on the heartstrings. But a butterfly helped too much may lack the wing power it needs to fly. It is in the trial that the strength is formed.

Change is hard. The disorder, the confusion, even simply the newness. Moving from one place to another, beginning or ending a relationship, graduating, starting or finishing a job, making or losing a friend, birthing or adopting a baby, aging, it all exacts a toll. During times of change, we may long for the safety and familiarity of stasis. I'll admit that I'd avoid the struggle at all costs if I could. I *like* stasis.

But change comes for us all.

For birds, conserving energy is paramount. It is a lot of work to be a bird, after all. This conservation goes into a higher gear at night, as songbirds and shorebirds and most raptors do the majority of their birdy tasks during the day. They gather food, find water, avoid predators, care for their feathers, communicate through chirps and songs. In season, they mate and nest and raise young. Except for migration, most birds sleep at night just like we do. Well, not *just* like we do.

After dusk, many birds, including some of the most active, like chickadees and swifts, and the largest, like turkey vultures, descend into torpor, a near-hibernation state. Their bodies cool and their metabolism slows, conserving calories—energy—for the day ahead. Other birds, like Mourning Doves, use torpor in times where food is lean. Still others, such as the hummingbird, use it to save energy, not only at night, but also while they rest mid-migration. Only one bird that we know of—the Common Poorwill—goes beyond torpor into full winter hibernation. The story is told that the explorers Lewis and Clark were the first to discover this, baffled by encountering a bird that certainly seemed asleep, but couldn't be awakened.

In torpor a bird's metabolic system slows down, requiring less energy to function. It's a bit like taking a day to lounge around the house instead of hiking up into the mountains—your body will need fewer calories to work well. But while in torpor, birds can be easy pickings for predators. Their reaction time is compromised by their lower body temperature, making their choice of roosting position and use of camouflage especially important.

Here's the other thing: If you see a bird—or another animal that falls into torpor, like a box turtle or a bumblebee—in this state, it will look like nothing is happening. It will look utterly inert, even dead.

But it isn't.

Before their winter rest, brown and black bears gain 20 to 40 percent of their body weight in fat storage. Pause and think about that for a second. If you are, say, a 150-pound adult, that'd be like putting on more than thirty pounds in a single autumn just by eating fish, meat, and berries. What a feat!

We commonly say that bears hibernate, but they never enter a true state of hibernation. Instead, they descend into torpor, just like the birds. While in this still state, they don't eat, drink, or defecate. Occasionally they'll shift position, lightly waking to get more comfortable. This torpor allows our northernmost brown and black bears to survive up to eight months without ingesting anything at all. (Polar bears typically do not hibernate.) During their winter sleep, which isn't a sleep per se, but an active suspension of sorts, the bears live off their body's reserves.

In *Hamilton*, Lin-Manuel Miranda talks about "lying in wait" rather than waiting. I love this image. In nature, torpor is preparation, not wasted time. A sleeping bear in its den will look dormant, but its body is metabolizing fat into food and water, the processes of digestion and oxygenation and blood flow all humming along, albeit slowly. The bear waits for spring when it will emerge leaner but strong, following the deep gift of rest that is written into the fabric of creation.

Even God rests, ceasing from the labor of creating the world on the seventh day.

"I'm in torpor," I tell Daryl, the blankets pulled up to my chin one chilly weekend morning. "I probably shouldn't get up today."

Weathering change will be nearly impossible without acquiescing to this holy pattern. Migrating hummingbirds don't just fly and fly and fly. They stop. They sleep. They recover. To survive the harsh winter months, bears fuel up and then hunker down. There is no shame in taking things slowly. In fact, at least once every week, God commands it of us all. And the more closely we look at the natural world, the more we will discover this rhythm everywhere.

For example, there is a unique window roughly four times per day in all of the world's oceans. For a moment, the push and pull of tides ceases and the water is still. Sediment settles. Dusky waters clear. Delicate animals emerge from shells and burrows. It's as if the seas exhale for a moment, stopping their relentless ebb and flow. It's called a *slack tide*, a brief pause in the strong currents that govern the ocean as they stand for a moment on the tipping point of the highest high tide or the lowest low. There are dangerous dives that can be made most safely within these short spans of time—minutes, usually, or very occasionally, hours.

I went scuba diving twice as a teenager, both times during a business trip my parents took my younger sister Caitlyn and me on to Bermuda. They put us in lessons so Dad could attend meetings and Mom could sit beachside with a book uninterrupted. Bermuda was so bonkers expensive and our family budget so tight that they let us know right off the bat that we'd be eating the hotel's free enormous continental breakfast and the trip's complimentary fancy restaurant dinners. In between, we would scrounge.

"Load up!" my dad told us at the buffet every morning, nudging us from our still unfinished first helpings to go back to the food line for a second round. "Load up!"

The first day, Cait and I wheedled a nine-dollar Cherry Coke out of my mom to split poolside at noon. The second, she hustled us through the breakfast line and into our swimsuits.

"It's scuba day!" she said. Even at the courageous age of seventeen, practicing in the hotel pool with the ocean just out of sight, I remember thinking, "There are an awful lot of ways to die doing this." We were warned about Portuguese Man o' War, jellyfish with a sting so painful it could—but probably wouldn't—kill you. They told us about fire coral, which would not kill you but certainly put you into so much pain that you'd wish you were dead. Though we wouldn't be diving very deep, we learned how to avoid the bends, air bubbles forced into the bloodstream of divers who surfaced too quickly. These would be excruciating and could also, of course, be fatal. Then there was the non-zero chance of drowning.

"I think I'm ready to be done with the scuba diving," I told my mom that evening.

"One more day," she said. "It'll be fun."

It didn't help that on that second day—the real ocean dive day—our guides kept cracking up about the barracuda they'd seen the day before.

"Followed one of the tourists around the whole time!" one guffawed in Bermuda's signature British accent, slapping a knee. "Must have been her perfume or something! Well, let's suit up." Caitlyn and I survived, she aglow and me afeared, but after my first open ocean diving experience, I happily hung up my fins for good.

Today I feel the same about scuba diving as I do about visiting Australia: It might look fun, but I'm certain I'd be dead within minutes. My Australian friend Ed calls this "a common misconception," but I think he's just trying to get us to visit his family in Perth. (Not happening, Ed. I have seen pictures of the funnel web spider.)

A person could, of course, go scuba diving *in Australia* and then be dead within seconds rather than minutes. Nota bene.

That said, in my vast scuba diving experience, I learned that one of the most important things to keep in mind is the rise and fall of the tides. Depending on the dive site, the pull of the current may matter a lot or very little, but there are magical underwater places on this earth that will straight up kill you—and have killed real, experienced divers— if you dive at any other time than a slack tide. Stasis is a gift. There are things that can only be accomplished during peaceful windows when it appears on the surface that nothing is happening. If we are on the lookout for them, lying in wait, ready to learn, poised to prepare, eyes open to wonder, magic can happen.

It's quiet in the eye of the hurricane, but it's also often quiet right before a change begins. Before migration—and often during rest stops along the journey—there is torpor. Before spring, there is a bear's long hibernation. Before the move there is one last walk through a silent, empty house. The marriage proposal occurs after days or weeks or months of planning and waiting, and then a final deep in-breath and a kneeling down. The tides pull and push, pull and push. But for a few brief windows every day, they stop.

Today, as I walk my two younger children to the front of the school for their first day of the academic year, Felicity entering kindergarten—*big school*—for the first time, we pause at the foot of the tall cement stairs for just a moment. I watch the first five-and-three-quarters years of her life flash through my mind in a blink. She was a baby *yesterday*, tucked next to my heart inside a fabric sling while I fixed dinner, her warm breath tickling my neck. But now she squeezes my hand, releases it, and skips ahead.

The wait only seems long until it ends.

3

Forests

Come forth into the light of things,
let nature be your teacher.

WILLIAM WORDSWORTH

I GREW UP ON THE EDGE of the Nicolet National Forest—now
known as the Chequamegon-Nicolet—a preserve that covers over sixty
thousand acres in northern Wisconsin. Only a handful of miles from
my house were wooded trails surrounding boggy lakes and more
wildlife than a National Geographic special. White-tailed deer were
ever-present, rambling out of the wilderness and into parks and yards.
In the fall, when they were in rut, deer would careen blindly onto the
highways that abutted their sanctuary. We only hit one during my youth,
smashing into an eight-point buck with the family sedan just as the
speed limit fortuitously dropped from sixty-five to forty, but our near-
misses numbered at least half a dozen every year. Deer were everywhere,
high-stepping through the snow, stripping bark off the trees, bedding
down under the shaggy branches of the neighborhood's pines.

Beyond those antlered cervids, there were chickadees and jays,
black bears and muskrat, beavers, grouse, river otters, foxes, fishers,
owls, woodpeckers, vireos, and raccoons. Once, out on a summer hike
with my sister, I put my shoulder against a little lean-to structure built
to keep firewood covered for the nearby warming hut and looked up
to see the shaggy, prickled tail of a porcupine hanging not even a foot

above my head. Recently both wolves and elk have also been reintroduced to the Nicolet, an effort to rewild the forests as they once were.

Forests have a texture to them, a smell. Shaggy hemlocks and
balsam fir trees abut swamps, bracken ferns carpet hillsides, white and
red pines grow where the ground begins to climb and dry. The trees
speak to each other through odors aboveground and roots and fungi
beneath. A forest is a community, every inch of soil brimming with
life. Dead trees lie upon the forest floor, slowly turning to soil and
filling the air with the odor of peat and rot.

Kneel down and you'll notice even more life at work, the understory
alive and alight with color, the activity of invertebrates, and the lush
life of smaller plants. Atop a northern Wisconsin forest floor with
properly draining soil, you'll find princess pine, six-inch prehistoric
plants that look like miniature trees. Their soft needles and convenient
size make them wonderful for Christmas wreaths or table garnishes
(as long as you're careful not to overharvest); they'll even take to a pot
on a sunny windowsill if you preserve their roots. Pocket-sized winter-
green plants spread their waxy green leaves to catch the hints of sun
that make it through the canopy, their red berries edible and their
leaves wonderful for teas. My sisters and I would pluck a leaf or two
and chew it as we hiked, its toothpaste-flavor filling our mouths with
a breeze. Turn over a dead log and, if you are very lucky, you might
glimpse the shine of a blue spotted salamander in the leaf litter.

In high school, my biology teacher sent my classmates and me out
to find fifty different leaves, the dreaded leaf collection assignment the
previous year's sophomores warned us about. We collectively bewailed
its impossibility. We knew of maple and oak and birch trees—the
maple mostly from the Canadian flag, the oaks because of the acorns
that rained down in autumn, the birch because their white bark was
too distinctive to possibly miss, even for the unobservant. But what
else was there? No evergreens were allowed, having needles rather
than leaves, making the project doubly impossible. I planned to grab
a sample from the ornamental crabapple tree in my parents' front yard,

bringing my total to four, but after that I was stumped. How would I come up with *fifty different leaves?*

"Stop bellyaching and go out into the forest," said Mr. Schaffer, tall and bearded and perpetually detached. "It's not like I'm asking you to bring me moon rocks." We eventually did go out, in ones and twos, to the Nicolet or the leafy expanse right behind the school or our own forested backyards. At first, we saw exactly what we expected—only the familiar maples and oaks and birches. We dutifully gathered these few leaves and then began to slowly notice that—wonder!—there were other species too. *Dozens* of them. Even the usual suspects weren't identical to one another, a fact we noticed as soon as we began looking more closely. The forest was alive and so much more diverse than I had ever believed. There were sugar maples and black maples, one smooth on the underside of its leaves, the other fuzzy. There were silver maples with deeper V-shapes in their leaf notches. One leaf I thought was a maple turned out to be an elm. The heart-shaped yellow leaf I found wasn't a birch at all, but a quaking aspen, sister to another variety found right in my backyard—the big-toothed aspen. I could see that one from my own bedroom window, I'd just never actually *seen* it before.

We filled our notebooks in short days, just a few hours squeezed in between hockey practice and band, football or cheerleading or theater rehearsals. And suddenly the forests began to look different to us, not because they had changed but because we had.

Trees bud at the end of autumn. Wait—what? I know. We expect buds in the spring. And indeed, that's when blossoms and new leaves and fruit begin to appear. But buds begin much earlier, a tree's last push at the end of the fall. During a season that ushers in showers of falling leaves, quiet fallowness, and the icy chill of winter's bite, trees are already preparing for the newness of spring. Each bud holds within it a leaf, shoot, or flower, protected from the plunging temperatures by a *bud scale*—small, modified leaves that form the arboreal equivalent of an insulated sleeping bag around the tender inner bud.

Look closely at an overwintering branch and you will see buds tightly closed, leaf scars from where those let go of their branches in autumn, and lenticels—pores in the outer bark that aid gas exchange. Facilitating the uptake of CO_2 allows the tree to perform photosynthesis, preparing even in the coldest months to supply spring growth. For this reason, lenticels are often clustered close to buds. This is where the energy will be needed. New growth takes fuel.

By mid-spring the blossoms feel inevitable, green, leafy growth springing up all over. But in early spring they ring miraculous: a rebirth, a resurrection. Winter seemed as though it would never end and then, somehow, it did. But this change, this seeming resilience is not miraculous, at least not in the sense that it has no logical explanation. The buds were there all along, prepared and tucked in for the dark months, readying themselves to burst open with the precious truth of spring: winter and its discomfort, its frozenness, its death, is not the story's end. It never is.

God promises us an ultimate transformation, the spring of resurrection, with Christ as the firstfruit of this reality. This act of transformation, spring's final triumph over winter's grip of death, will happen quickly. In Scripture it is described as lightning racing across the sky. Yet its instantaneous occurrence belies the reality that this metamorphosis has been millennia in the making.

It began in a garden eons ago.

Back in the spring of 2010, I was searching for my first pastoral call. I sat in my final seminary courses with an open laptop, staring at the Presbyterian Church's job boards. Our church-and-clergy matching system works a bit like online dating: Churches and pastoral candidates both post profiles and then they are matched according to strengths and needs. Candidates can also self-refer, as can churches.

Daryl had begun a PhD program at Vanderbilt in Tennessee, while I finished my degree in New Jersey. We were eager for a geographical reunion after nine months of living in two separate states, so I limited my church search to within an hour of Nashville. "Surely this will be easy," I thought. "It's Nashville! There's a church on every corner!" But once I was finally cleared to begin looking—it's bad manners to search for a call before all the required ordination boxes are ticked by passing exams and such—I was shocked. There were simply no opportunities for a first-call pastor. Every open position required five to ten years of experience. So I waited and fretted, prayed and fretted, lamented to friends and fretted. The question I woke to every morning and fell asleep to every night was an anxious one: What if there was nothing out there for me?

Often the hardest part of preparation is that we don't know what exactly we're preparing for, or when. I fought frustration, impatience, despair. Change doesn't always come to us with clarity. There are seasons when all we know is that *something* is going to change—we just don't yet know what.

What I didn't see—couldn't see—was that God was at work at a church in rural Wisconsin that had just lost its pastor. The congregation was following the denominational requirements for putting together a mission study, listening to one another, and hiring an interim. They were not officially on the job market yet—and even if they had been, I would have missed them since I was not looking in Wisconsin. My reasoning was logically sound—Daryl and I had lived apart long enough—but it missed several crucial elements. It lacked an openness to change beyond the limits I'd imposed. It assumed that God's call would fall on my timeline. It purposefully ignored the deep and unfortunate truth that it is often struggle and not ease that God uses to prepare us for what lies ahead. It is true in our lives, and it is true in our forests as well. As Aldo Leopold notes in *A Sand County Almanac*, "It is a curious circumstance that only pines in full sunlight are bitten by weevils; shaded pines are ignored. Such are the hidden uses of adversity."

If I could go back and speak to that twenty-seven-year-old near-graduate, I would tell her to embrace her dormant days with courage. To expand her vision. To trust God in the waiting and the preparation and the mist. To not assume that the Almighty would—or should—do her precise bidding. Mostly I'd encourage her to take some deep breaths, shut that laptop, and tune in to the last bits of graduate school in front of her because if a new position *did* open up and she applied to it within the first thirty seconds she wouldn't appear qualified as much as she would seem overeager and perhaps a little unhinged.

Daryl and I joke that when we're really anxious about an impending change, it's like we've climbed a tree and are clinging to the spindly branches at the top yelling, carrying on, and waving our arms around. "I'm not in my tree anymore," we'll tell one another when our fears have settled. We've climbed down and we can, once again, see the path ahead more clearly.

I've begun to think less about myself up there in that treetop and more about which metaphorical tree I'm climbing in the first place. What if I climbed up into the branches of Jesus? What if, amid the painful process of waiting, with the open wound of impending, uncertain change, and in seasons of lengthy preparation, we could find our way back to the source of hope?

As a teenager I spent part of each of summer at HoneyRock, a Christian summer camp located just half an hour from my house. As part of each week's experience, campers and their counselors would leave their cabins and the centralized bathrooms with their flushing toilets and hot water and either hike or canoe out into the Nicolet. Into the wilderness.

Most of my cabinmates were girls from the Chicago suburbs, Wheaton or Naperville or Elmhurst, all with trendier jeans but far less forest experience than I had. I felt brave and bold with my knowledge of the basic flora and fauna, the ways the counselors—often city kids themselves, and only a handful of years older than I was—relied upon me to help find the trail.

There came a moment every summer when I'd pull out the map from my pack, look at the lakes and forests, and feel a sense of placement and knowledge and trust.

"We're headed north," I'd say. "And if we can canoe around this big bend in the Eagle River before dusk, we will pull up to my parents' pier. I bet they'll even make us dinner." Often those canoe trips were filled with rain and wind; the hikes were always bedeviled by ticks and humidity and mosquitoes. But then we'd turn the corner in the Eagle River, make it past the nest of the Bald Eagles in the white pines that lined the eastern shore of Yellow Birch Lake, and there in the bay just beyond I would see the rust-colored pier. The sign of home.

Change is hard, friends. We know it. We've lived it. And yet amid all the uncertainty and newness, our roots may hold. Because for all Scripture tells and teaches about change, it also reminds us of a deep and abiding truth: *Jesus Christ is the same yesterday, today, and forever.*

This is our compass and our anchor, our refuge and our salvation. We will be changed. We *are* being changed. However much we choose to prepare, there will still be unexpected bumps in the road. It can all be very painful and scary and difficult and unsettling. But even amidst the heady transformations that we will endure, one thing remains.

And he is so very, very good.

4

Fledging

*In the stillness of the quiet, if we listen, we can
hear the whisper of the heart giving strength to
weakness, courage to fear, hope to despair.*

HOWARD THURMAN

THE HOUSE FINCHES in our backyard have left the nest. Three of them have survived the dangerous days of nestling-hood and are now learning how to be real, grown-up birds. They are fledging. Today they're perching on our string lights and begging their exhausted parents for food. Birds grow remarkably quickly, going from newly hatched to nearly adult-sized in a matter of days or weeks. By the thirteenth day after breaking through their shells, House Finches are fully feathered, though they will not be strong fliers for a few more days to come.

I watch one of the fledglings atop the backyard lights, her new feathers sticking up like an overslept teenager's hair. She squawks impatiently as her father hustles to fill her open beak. After House Finches fledge, it is the father who continues to feed them for a couple more weeks. Mom will be off building a new nest for their next brood. House Finches are quite prolific, often raising three or more clutches in a single year. The fledgling swallows and yells again. Their father-daughter ballet gives me pause. The youngster is only a few centimeters shy of her father in height and, by my eye, just a fraction of an ounce short of his weight. But she is not yet ready to be fully out on her own, finding food, dodging cats and hawks, doing that undulating roller coaster flight that House Finches do. She still wants her sustenance provided to her.

Dad Bird obliges, bringing her one snack and then another. I can't see what he is feeding her, though I notice he isn't simply pulling seeds from the feeder that hangs only a few feet away. House Finches love seeds, but they eat grain, buds, and fruit too. Perhaps he is plying her with bits of plant material that are easier to digest. He pauses, resting a beat as she cries for more. Then he hops to the ground and glances up at her, as if to say, "There's food right here, so maybe you could try getting it yourself?" She protests all the more. I'm anthropomorphizing now, but I promise I nearly see him sigh. He grabs another beakful from the grass and heads back, once again, to her side.

Upheaval, whether expected or unexpected, is stressful. Big Girl House Finch has never needed to feed herself before. For her entire two-week life, her parents brought meals directly to her. But she is a baby no longer, and it is time to learn the adult habits of feeding that will sustain her for the years to come. Still, she is resistant. Bewildered.

It's no wonder. What's a challenge for fledglings is often a challenge for us as well. Change disrupts our habits, forcing us to forge novel neural pathways. New beginnings can be, and often are, exhausting and even frightening. Of course we resist.

Poet Christian Wiman writes that "to be conscious is to be conscious of suffering." This is one of the unique struggles of change too. It wakes us from our sleepwalking and jars us into awareness, requiring us to feel. Often what we experience will be discomfort, fear, or even pain. Change, even good or necessary change, brings with it the grief of loss.

Plus, we can't always prepare for change, since much of it will be unexpected. The red squirrel devours acorns to put on weight, preparing for the expected seasonal transition, but she doesn't foresee that a Blue Jay will find her winter cache or a fox stake out the ground beneath her favorite branch. We, too, will face much unanticipated change. Still, what we *can* ready ourselves for is the reality that there will be change. Flux is certain. The more we can prepare ourselves for that, the better.

I'm sitting at the kitchen table responding to church emails. Daryl has just taken the kids to school and it's Tuesday, the day that I usually work from home. I type a bit, research a bit, and then I am writing some more when I hear a skittering. A little brown house mouse freezes in the middle of the floor before turning tail and scurrying back under the dryer.

House mice are so sweet and pastoral when they remain outdoors, perfect illustrations for children's storybooks. They build nests for their young, lined with soft materials: grasses, sawdust, and bits of fabric. They don't fledge, exactly, but their young are fully furred at ten days old and leave the nest for good on day twenty-one. In those three short weeks they go from newly born, naked and blind, to capable of doing everything an adult mouse can do. They prepare quickly. They must.

Mice are also, unfortunately, potential disease vectors when they wander too close to people. We faced an infestation of them during the pandemic, with Covid-19 shutdowns creating ideal conditions for small rodents to thrive. The day I discovered them, Daryl was down with the shingles virus, bedridden and racked with so much pain he could barely speak. The de-mousing fell to me.

"Where there is one mouse, there are ten," a friend told me, and the phrase has haunted me ever since. It proved true then, mouse after mouse showing up in the hall bathroom, the kitchen, the garage, until I thought I might lose my mind. I stood bleary at the sink one morning, having slept fitfully in the living room because Daryl couldn't bear to even brush against me in sleep, the shingles sending electric shocks of nerve pain radiating across his torso. Trying to get my bearings, praying for the strength to face our two-, four-, and seven-year-old on my own for the fifth day in a row, to keep up my shambling attempts at pandemic homeschooling, offering my best approximation of normalcy in the middle of a global catastrophe, I suddenly felt something icy cold skitter across my bare foot. A mouse, of course. To be honest, I still haven't recovered.

Today, I set out a handful of glue traps and immediately feel a pang of ethical discomfort. The death of animals is a constant and macabre part of creation after the fall. We are no longer in Eden and the signs abound. These glue traps are safer for our kids then the snap traps and we've also found them to be more effective, but they're cruel. A mouse stuck in the glue can struggle and suffer for days before succumbing to dehydration or suffocation. It is a drawn-out, horrible way to go. But now it's time to turn to my pastoral care calls to the families displaced by the current fires, and so I put it out of my mind.

The traps sit empty for a week, and I'm hopeful the invader has left us for the great outdoors. But then the following Tuesday, I'm home again. The fires that had forced evacuations for some of our congregants are under control and the skies are clear once more. An air of optimism has descended on our little neighborhood. We're going to make it through this round. We're going to be okay.

Then I hear it. A faint, frantic squeaking, sounds of desperation and fear. I know before I even look that we've caught it. I get a trash bag and go to the trap, reminding myself not to look, but I can't help it. The mouse is sable brown with translucent pink ears, its feet peach-colored and impossibly tiny. It is stuck by each foot, its tail, and its furred belly but also—and here my breath catches—the tip of its nose. It looks at me out of wet, black eyes, snuffling so gently that its breath sounds like a plea. There's no saving it now—the glue trap has done its work. It's only a matter of time. A better person would take the mouse outside and crush it beneath a boot to end its misery. A *much* better person wouldn't have set glue traps at all. But I stuff the whole mess into a trash bag, cinch the top, and put it into the bin outside.

I hear its plea at night as I try to fall asleep. I see its eyes.

"Please," it asks me. "Please."

To be a person is to participate in suffering. We experience it. We receive it. Worst of all, we cause it. Our words and actions ripple out to the edges of our world, concentric circles of good and evil, blessing and destruction. We are agents of change, every one of us, and we can't always predict what a hurried word or a careless oversight might do. Part of the pain of being human is navigating this near-constant fog of ambiguity, of leaving behind the certainties of childhood and entering the moral mist of adulthood.

Listen, writes the apostle Paul in the book of 1 Corinthians, *I tell you a mystery: We will not all sleep, but we will all be changed—in a flash, in the twinkling of an eye, at the last trumpet. For the trumpet will sound, the dead will be raised imperishable, and we will be changed.* This change is the replacement of our mortal, frail, finite bodies with immortal ones, healed and whole and strong and well. But it will also, I think, lift the fog. A world of suffering and death, confusion and groping about in the dark will be overcome by one of renewal and peace and understanding and light. This final change will usher in an eschaton where God will wipe every tear from our eyes and there will be no more pain—the pain we've suffered, the pain we've caused.

This is the change we long for as we experience the ache of so much difficult change here and now. As we are faced with heart-rending decisions, with impossible choices big and small. This divinely promised change is the hoped-for one that I cling to and prepare for as pastor and parent and daughter and friend, trusting that this good and beautiful and wrecked and ravaged world will not be our ultimate end, but that it will open up into something even better. That one day our frail race will be stripped of its brutality and infighting and lies and war and suffering and infused with all the life of the Spirit. The ultimate change. Our final transformation.

We will fledge.

Here is something paradoxical that I've learned: When we expect change to be hard, this strangely makes it easier. This type of contradiction shows up frequently in Scripture: *those who lose their lives will find them; blessed are those who mourn; the last will be first.* Perhaps it shouldn't surprise us that weathering change hinges on such an absurdity too. In the kingdom of God all is topsy-turvy according to the world because the world is so often interested in power and influence and control while God is interested only in that which will last: faith, hope, love.

Preparing for the difficulty of change—even when that preparation is as simple as acknowledging that the change may be difficult—can be a great help in navigating it well. When our children go back to school in the fall, we expect that those first couple of weeks—a new routine, teacher, classes—will be challenging. Leaving a church can be as painful as grieving a death. The evolution of a friendship can sow confusion and anguish. Feeling these feelings, making space for them, and honoring them can help us be gentle with ourselves amid tough transitions. No one gets a medal for pretending change doesn't hurt.

Speaking of change, it's a day later and the House Finches are at it again—dad and daughter. He is trying, once more, to teach her to find her own food. She is, once more, yelling at him from atop our backyard string lights, in hopes that he will deliver her meal straight to her waiting mouth. They are so strangely alluring, House Finches. Everything about them looks rough-hewn, from their thick beaks to their brown feathers to their angular tails. I watch as they come to a stalemate. Dad hops to the ground and pulls a mouthful full of food from the lawn, holding the seeded grasses up so his daughter can clearly see them. It would be easier to simply keep feeding her in the short term, but he understands what she doesn't yet—that he won't always be there to provide for her. Mama bird will need her partner to bring food for their next clutch of helpless nestlings. This daughter will soon be on her own.

The fledgling bird watches her father. She calls out angrily once, twice. They stare one another down and I watch her weigh her decision, frozen, unsure.

Then she flits to the ground.

Big changes can rock our world, leaving us breathless and unsure. In *Masters of Change*, Stulberg describes "something that fundamentally shifts our experience of ourselves and the world we inhabit, sometimes for better and sometimes for worse" as a "disorder event." Examples include everything from making a friend to recovering from an accident to grieving the death of a loved one. According to his research, the average person goes through "thirty-six disorder events in the course of their adulthood—or about one every eighteen months. This does not include aging, the ever-present, ongoing disorder event that many of us futilely resist and deny." (More on that in chapter seven.)

We can feel this down to our bones, can't we? Think of the disorder events of your life—moves, a new job, world events, romantic relationships, changes in parenting, unexpected injuries or accidents. Now think about how those disruptions made you *feel*. For me, disruptive change most often brings a combination of feeling bereaved and aggrieved. I am sad, but also angry. I wonder why, when everything seemed stable and fine, this monkey wrench was thrown into the mix. I'm frustrated at being knocked off-course. I'm unsettled. Confused. None of those feelings are pleasant. I'm willing to bet that many of your disorder-related feelings are similarly unwelcome. It can make us want to stave off change at every opportunity.

Yet this is simply impossible. Stulberg makes the point that, while most of us think that "change and disorder are the exceptions," exactly the opposite is true. He writes, "In reality, they are the rules. . . . Life *is* flux." We move from order to disorder to reorder time and time again. In Scripture, we see the cycle of birth, sin, and redemption. We watch our own lives echo the story of Jesus—life, death, and resurrection—in countless ways, both big and small. We work a full day—*life*—climb into bed at night—*death*—and wake the next—*resurrection*. On a macro level, we each live awaiting the final change we will experience in this world—physical death—and our promised hope of life eternal, healed and whole.

The Bible illustrates that life is a journey of transformation. As we travel from age to age and place to place, we will only frustrate ourselves if our hope is to remain the same or, after facing disorder, to return to our previous sameness. Abraham was changed by God. Moses, Miriam, Esther, and Deborah all left their encounters with the Almighty as different people. The fledgling will learn to feed herself. There is no going back.

This does not mean that change always happens quickly. Sometimes it comes in an instant, but more often it is a process. A long and often painful one. The myth in Christian circles is that all Jesus-related change happens at the moment of divine connection—lost and then found, blind and then seeing, ill and then *poof!* healed and whole. Yet as we read Scripture's stories of conversion, we discover that transformation most often follows divine encounters in fits and starts. Peter opens his heart to the Gentiles *years* after meeting Jesus. Paul's abrasive arrogance doesn't evaporate in a simple second when he accepts Christ's call to follow him. As the Plush Horse tells his long-eared friend in *The Velveteen Rabbit*, the transition from toy to real isn't instantaneous. *You become.*

When we make a decision to get on the path, to turn from our own way, we are freed from sin and made perfect in Christ. Justified. And it is also in that moment that the ongoing inner work, that of sanctification, truly begins. We haven't arrived; we've simply set foot on the path. Yet this path is where the entire journey will take place, with all of its surprising uphills and downhills to come.

It's nearly impossible to gauge all the after-effects of change in the moment.

The dust needs to settle first.

Curiosity:

approaching newness with open-minded interest.

Curiosity enables us to receive novel information without defensiveness, fear, or judgment. Think of how a house cat might react when you turn on a nature documentary: a tilt of the head, dilated pupils, intense but unafraid interest. Cats epitomize curiosity—the focused, open-minded desire to know more.

Curiosity helps us practice attentiveness, asking questions of ourselves, others, and our circumstances as we seek to discern what our next steps might be.

5

Noticing

I want to state unequivocally what the beautiful is not.
It is not cute. It is not easy. It is not banal. . . .
And it's not unthreatening.

BARBARA NICOLOSI

As a college student, I spent a semester studying at Oxford through a consortium program. I took a few seminar-style classes, but mostly my time was spent going to tutorials—one-on-one instruction— at the row home of an English poetry professor. He wasn't so much eccentric as he was an unmade bed, his hair wild, shirt buttons askew, glasses smudged, and one sweater layered over several others to ward off Britain's signature dampness. He sported a five o'clock shadow and a perpetually furrowed brow.

The professor's brick flat was as tidy as he was not, lined with bookshelf after bookshelf of snug paperbacks and heavy bound volumes, his kitchen a perfect dollhouse version of America's typical sprawling ones. He'd offer me tea and I'd always say yes, since yes seemed to be the polite thing to say, and then I'd spend our hour together trying my best to choke down every drop of the piping cup, its bitterness leaden upon my soda-spoiled palate.

I brought the professor rumpled essays that we would workshop together, sitting in his stately armchairs as the anemic English sun shone through the blinds. I wrote creative, cheeky nonfiction about the wilds of northern Wisconsin and the people I'd grown up with there. I'd read aloud to him as he drank his tea and made his notes, stopping me occasionally to interject or ask a question. Every once in a while, my reading was interrupted with a *bang*, as he'd pull a paperback off the shelf just above his head and throw it at his cat.

"No, Tilda!" he'd yell. "Not on the furniture!"

One day, sitting in my armchair and choking down the tea of hospitality, I read to him that Lake Superior was the same size as Scotland. *Bang*. I looked up. It wasn't a book thrown at Tilda this time. He'd stomped both his feet on the floor.

"Absolutely not," he said. "That cannot be true."

"I might be wrong," I said, having learned some academic humility. "Maybe we can check?" He pulled a heavy atlas off a shelf and opened it on his lap, turning pages until he got to the United States. He looked at the legend for scale, found the lake in question, and then flipped over to Scotland.

"Oh my God," he said, staring down at the page. "Oh my God." He then dismissed me just ten minutes into our scheduled hour.

"I need to ponder this," he said. "I had no idea."

Noticing can stop us in our tracks. A new perspective, new realization, or new encounter can change the way we understand the world. It may bring us to our knees with delight or anguish. Sometimes it will drive us to wonder. To prayer. Even to faith.

One October I visited the Cape May Birding Festival in New Jersey, advertised delightfully with the tagline: *So. Many. Birds.* A migratory cul-de-sac, the Cape May Peninsula sticks out into the Atlantic in perfect fashion for songbirds to pause, deciding whether they want to brave the twelve miles of ocean that will take them to the other side of the Delaware Bay or turn inland instead, heading north to skirt the shore with its food and shelter before returning south again. Raptors and shorebirds, have no compunction about such a long flight over water. They forge ahead.

As I stood at Morning Flight, the viewing spot for this phenomenon, beside a couple of world-class guides and a few dozen fellow bird tourists, I kept wanting to call foul.

"Eastern Meadowlark," said the head guide, pointing to one individual bird in a sea of dozens of Yellow-rumped Warblers, each of which was so far above us that it looked no bigger than a speck of pepper spilled on a tablecloth.

"No way," I said. "You can't possibly identify it from here." The bird flew closer. I raised my binoculars. He was correct.

"How on earth do you do that?" I asked.

"Practice."

He pointed out Red-winged Blackbirds, Palm Warblers, Tree Swallows, Eastern Phoebes. He picked a Black-and-white Warbler out of another sea of Yellow-rumps a hundred feet above us, all in the cloudy, barely there light of dawn. Also, it was raining.

"No seriously," I asked again. "How?"

He walked me through the process, noting that beginning birders tended to look first for color, which is hard to make out in poor visibility or at great distances. He spoke to us about flight patterns, body shape, vocalizations. Each bird has a flight signature, the species equivalent of a fingerprint. Put those things together and you could identify almost any bird from far away and in bad light.

"Plus seriously, it's just practice," he said. "I've been doing this for a long time." Trained counters stand at Morning Flight for over a month each autumn, beginning their days in the darkness of predawn, tallying every bird that passes by. We bird tourists stood on a wooden platform raised just above the tree line, while the official counter stood on the ridge above us, a protection against distraction by well-meaning but occasionally noisy amateurs.

"I was the main counter here for years," the guide told us, noting that he'd be up on the ridge in all kinds of weather five or six days a week for hours. "Then I'd go to work for the rest of the day. I didn't see my wife much."

The Cape May trip reinvigorated my own birding practice. Before witnessing how keen our guides' powers of observations were, I had no idea that type of insight and distance identification was even possible. It gave me something to reach for, to aspire to. I began to attend to birds' shapes and silhouettes and sounds, not just their colors. I began to fall in love with flight signatures. I leaned into Mary Oliver's observation that to pay attention is our honest and proper work, seeking to tune in to that which I'd never noticed before.

It turns out that we can begin to learn how to see things we didn't even know to look for when someone helps open our eyes. As Annie Dillard notes, "Nothing on earth is more gladdening than knowing we must roll up our sleeves and move back the boundaries of the humanly possible once more." There is always, *always* more to notice.

If the gentle curiosity of noticing what is outside and around us is one key to weathering change, tuning our attention to what is happening internally can be more transformative still.

"You seem like you're struggling," Daryl will gently remark to me on occasion. Often our inner states speak louder to others than they do to ourselves. Those who love us well can usually tell if we're out of sorts or troubled or angry or afraid. But looking at our own inner mirrors, learning to see ourselves as we are and not turn away, can be quite a challenge.

"Do you want to take a walk and figure it out?" he'll ask, and I'll retreat to the birds and the trails. A few blocks away, I often discover that yes, I am struggling. Struggling with the weight of responsibilities at church or at home, the pace of change, my own thwarted plans. I am struggling and Daryl and Jesus and the kids all knew it, I just couldn't yet see it for myself.

In the book of Numbers, Moses brings God's people out of Egypt and into the wilderness where they wander for forty years. He is a shepherd-turned-leader, moving from familiar pastoral solitude to clamoring desert crowds, a difficult and significant change in and of itself. Plus: sheep don't complain, and people definitely do.

"I cannot carry all these people by myself!" Moses laments to God. *"The burden is too heavy for me."* His very next sentence gives us an intimate glimpse into the heart of an overwhelmed leader: *"If this is how you are going to treat me, please go ahead and kill me."* Moses has moved past curiosity and well into despair.

God responds to him by providing help—seventy elders to share the burden. Moses had tried to go it alone—in times of unexpected transition, we often do—but he needed help scaling up. Growth can be just as challenging as loss when it comes to change. When things expand, it will take us time to adjust to new ways of managing. Our old habits and patterns won't serve us well—or even be possible!— when we are faced with new metrics of size. Much is made of the pain of church decline, but church growth presents its own raft of difficulties.

But being curious about change is one of the postures that can help us weather it well. When we ask questions of ourselves and others and practice openness rather than retreat, attack, or defense, we will find ourselves better connected to the source of all life. And even when Moses explodes in exasperation, God does not chastise him for his earnest prayer of frustration. Instead God meets him by granting him the help that he needs. God is there for us in the same way, present to us in any change we might face.

The psalms are a masterclass in how learning to discover how our joy or fear or sadness or fury can help us connect with God. The psalm writers don't censor their grief or their rage. They dare to question not only the pain of human existence but the Almighty too. They frame the rigors of the human experience, including the difficulties inherent in life's many transitions, with honest personal reflection.

My soul is downcast within me, the psalmist laments. *Why have you forgotten me?* These difficult emotions are not kept hidden—they are written, spoken, sung, and shared. Paying mind to these deep places in our souls is what some faith leaders refer to as "holy attention." It is not selfish or indulgent to take stock of our hearts, noticing that which weighs us down or buoys us up, confuses or frightens us, turns us to worry. It is often the first step in discovering what we need to be able to continue.

I've begun to learn, after over a decade and a half of professional ministry and nearly twenty years of marriage, that when someone comes at me hot with emotion—anger, especially—it is unwise to lead with defensiveness. It's tempting, of course, a natural response to another's unexpected intensity. But it's almost always unhelpful in both the short and the long term. Instead, I try to practice curiosity, asking measured, gentle questions.

"This seems important to you," I'll say. "Can you help me understand your feelings around it?" In my better moments, I use this same kind practice on myself.

"You're really upset about this, Courtney," I'll probe. "Would you like to explore why?" Curiosity is a sacred discipline. Plus, the uncomfortable truth is that it is difficult to know God if we don't also seek to know ourselves.

"Let me know Thee who knowest me, let me know Thee even as I am known," prayed Saint Augustine, acknowledging the intimate way these two types of wisdom intertwine.

In addition, it can be achingly hard to process change if we haven't yet sorted through the big feelings it is bringing up within us. Noticing is a kindness, both to us and to others. It helps us gather information, pause for a breath, and take stock before bumbling full steam ahead, fueled by assumptions that may not be helpful or even true.

Noticing isn't just about paying attention to our difficult feelings, however. (Thank goodness!) The more we notice about the world around us, the more likely we are to experience awe. What a delightful emotion awe is. It's wonder mixed with delight and seasoned with surprise. It can transform not only our minds but our bodies too. Awe doesn't necessarily need to be tied to earth-shattering realizations. Simply noticing beauty and wonder in our backyards, on our streets, and in the faces of our neighbors can be a start to a lower stress baseline. The lower our stress, the easier it is for us to lean into learning, health, and growth.

The Memory and Aging Center at the University of California, San Francisco performed an experiment on older adults, a demographic that tends to struggle with loneliness and depression. Participants were instructed to go on a fifteen-minute walk each week and then take a selfie to document their experience. The moods of those in the control group improved a bit. This was unsurprising. We have all come to know that walking is good for us, whether we do it regularly or not.

But here is the twist: The experimental group was instructed to go on a walk—same length, same frequency—and while they did, to look specifically for things that brought them awe. In the end, those in the awe group "experienced significant boosts in their daily experience of positive prosocial emotions such as compassion and gratitude." Their depression faded more extensively. Also, the selfies they were asked to take showed themselves as smaller and smaller parts of the overall photo over time. The awe group began wanting to feature the beauty of the world around them—a pictorial example of the wonder they'd experienced.

As researcher Virginia Sturm wrote, "One of the key features of awe is that it promotes what we call 'small self,' a healthy sense of proportion between your own self and the bigger picture of the world around you."

This is why we linger at sunsets, plant flowers, and walk breathlessly up mountainsides. We long to be stretched beyond the mundane, to see beauty, to notice the wild world right at our fingertips. Our souls are hungry for encounters with the transcendent, and God has planted seeds of transcendence on every hill and valley. Curiosity about what is at play within our own minds is healthy, but an overemphasis on self-knowledge can run the risk of curving us inward. Wonder—particularly wonder at the natural world—is the counterbalance to too much naval gazing.

I once watched a PBS news story about Margaret Renkl, whose book *The Comfort of Crows* had just been released. The book is a collection of essays that weave in the wonders of nature with themes of aging, conservation, family history, faith, and hope. While reading it, I'd become enamored with the descriptions of her backyard, magic under each flower, wonders woven around the trunk of every tree.

But when I watched the news clip—filmed in her yard—what I noticed first was that it was just a yard. A nice, sprawling, central Tennessee backyard, but still—just a suburban yard. I realized then that the magic might be—must be!—present in my own backyard too. The difference was that Renkl had learned how to see.

On my birds-and-hope podcast, *The Thing with Feathers*, I asked Renkl how we might train ourselves to see the wonder in seemingly ordinary places like she does. In yards that are just yards. She responded,

> I think we almost had to . . . unlearn it, because I think children have it. I think we are all born capable of spending thirty minutes contemplating an anthill or staring out at the window and watching birds bring nesting materials to a hole in a tree or a crack in a brick building or around the metal frame of a warehouse window. We *can* do that, but somehow, we've lost the knack.

It is the great tragedy of adulthood, that much of what we grow up into—progress, efficiency, consumerism—will greatly impoverish us if we don't learn to set it back down. Yet what is lost as we leave childhood, our senses of awe and wonder and *seeing*, can often also be found again.

The way children experience the world can be reclaimed to us. Kids pay attention. They harbor an innate curiosity about the world. They also walk through life largely unhurried, awake to the magic of creature and creation. When our oldest son was just a toddler, I'd bewail how long it took us to get the single block from our condo to our car.

"Does he have to examine every *leaf*?" I asked Daryl, arriving late to a meeting once again, papers flying and shirt untucked. I see now that I was rushing one of my very best teachers.

It was the mystic Simone Weil who wrote that "absolutely unmixed attention is prayer." To focus in on the person right in front of us, the leaf, the blade of grass, the pattering of raindrops, the wound, the meal, the breeze, makes way for a divine encounter. Pulled as we are in every direction, sometimes it is the pain of change that becomes the shock of cold water to open our eyes.

When they became fully awake, they saw his glory, we read in Luke's Gospel. Peter, James, and John have walked up onto a mountain with Jesus. They are drowsy—it was a *long* walk, after all, and steep. Following Jesus has meant leaving hearth and home and comfort and safety behind. They are usually tired. They are often hungry. I am reminded of Teresa of Avila's anguished prayer after a cold, perilous journey: "If this is how you treat your friends, Lord, no wonder you have so few!"

These three disciples are weary. So very, very weary. Everything about their lives as they knew them has changed. But in this moment, their eyes are opened and they see Jesus as he is. In his glory, his splendor, his radiance. They wonder: Is this the same Jesus who has walked among them all this time? How could they have failed to notice?

Peter begins to babble incoherently, as Peter is wont to do. The other two disciples remain silent. Their eyes burn as they look upon clothing bright as lightning, but they cannot look away. They have arrived at one of the *thin places,* transcendent moments where the veil between the ordinary and sacred is pulled back just a little and we catch a glimpse of what lies beyond.

This is my Son whom I have chosen, a voice speaks from heaven. *Listen to him.*

We may long for such a voice from heaven—surely, we would listen then!—but more often we are recipients of the subtler signs of God's glory. A bloom in spring. A dragonfly paused upon the pier. The aurora borealis over a frozen field. The soft cheek of a child. The extended hand of forgiveness.

As we begin to notice these small miracles, to take them in, we too will be transformed.

6

Ecotones

We come to the water's edge when
what we hold cannot be contained.

BARBARA MAHANY

FIRST PRESBYTERIAN WAS my first pastorate, and one I'd accepted without any intention of ever leaving. I'd always admired Eugene Peterson, who pastored the same church in Bel Air, Maryland, for twenty-nine years. My friend Brian told the first church he served that he'd be there for at least ten years—and he was. Pastors can be a transient sort, but it's often those who stay put for a decade or more that end up having the most fruitful ministry. This had always been my plan. Still, staying put is often the exception and not the rule. In late 2013, after three years of life and ministry, together Daryl and I discerned that it was time to move on from our beloved church in Wisconsin.

Transferring to a new church, whether as a pastor, a member of the staff, or a congregant, isn't always a choice. Sometimes pastors get run out of town on a rail by congregations resistant to change; other times they are removed due to their own bad behavior. (And rightfully so!) Any of us—pastors and congregants alike—may move on for reasons that have nothing to do with a church's fit: A spouse may take a job in another city, children may need more than a local school system can provide, aging parents may require care three states away. Sometimes a departure is riddled with grief: There's been hurt or an uncovering of differences in values or belief. Nothing is certain besides the fact that Jesus will never leave us. The makeup of a congregation will change year upon year.

Still, I had hoped to be the pastoral exception in what can be a migratory profession. I'm loyal to a fault, the stubborn blood of my German ancestors thick in my veins. But it wasn't just loyalty. I'd fallen in love with this church, this town, these people. We'd built something astonishing together, the decades of their faithfulness and hardiness combined with the greenhorn energy of a young pastor determined to give it her all. To even consider leaving felt like the beginning of a death. I wasn't sure how I'd see it through. Yet as the days turned into weeks, Daryl and I had both begun to feel a similar leading.

Some of our decision was practical. He'd be done with his PhD coursework soon and ready to begin a vocation of his own. Clinton had little need for systematic theologians, and though the congregation and I had worked hard to get our little church budget into the black, we were eons away from being big enough to afford a second pastor.

But other concerns were of a spiritual nature: I'd begun sensing God leading us *away from* rather than *toward*. I felt both blessing and release in the work I'd done at this white clapboard parish, even as I was beginning to see that the hard truth they would need someone whose experience outweighed my own to take them the next mile.

As I slowly began putting out feelers to positions within other congregations, a man named Steve Yamaguchi called me to chat. Steve was then the Executive Presbyter (that's Presbyterian-speak for *Area Director*) of a Southern California Presbytery (that's Presbyterian-speak for *collection of churches*). The only problem was I could barely hear him over the roar of something in the background.

"Oh, I'm sorry!" he said. "I'm down at the ocean and the train just went by." When the noise faded, I asked if he took a lot of his calls at the beach. We were just turning the corner into a brittle, cold autumn in Wisconsin and I admitted to him that I was not *not* jealous. He laughed.

"Walking the shore has become a spiritual practice of mine," he said. "I'm here at least once a week." Though I lived far from the ocean, I knew this pull to liminal, transitional spaces, particularly in times of uncertainty or indecision. As a teenager I'd take the wooded path behind my house down to the lake and sit out on the dock or nestle in the hammock until the mosquitoes drove me back inside. As a pastor those years in Clinton, when things got overwhelming—four funerals in a month or a skirmish on the church board, a budget shortfall or a sermon that just wouldn't come together—I'd drive up the curving road to the cemetery on the outskirts of town, churning past farmland until I arrived at a rocky forest with a creek burbling through it. In winter I'd watch the hushed earth, the glints of sun on the crusts of snow that seemed to light them aglow from within like diamonds. In spring, I'd sit in my car with the windows down and my prayerbook in my lap, watching the prairie phlox and the yellow coneflowers bob in the breeze. In summer I'd get out and wander, finding quietness and peace in an overlap of forest and meadow with running water cutting a swath of life right down its middle.

Ecologists call these transitional spaces, places where two habitats change from one to the next—beach-to-ocean, for example, forest-to-wetland, or a wooded cemetery with a creek running through it—*ecotones*. Some ecotones feature a gradual shift from one habitat to another—a rich prairie will usually become a bit boggy over ten or twenty or a hundred yards before becoming a full-on swamp. Others feature a sharp distinction: where a forest ends and a creek begins. Mangroves are ecotones, as are estuaries and tidal flats.

Ecotones typically feature characteristics from both habitats, serving as an overlapping meeting point for plants and animals from each. This makes them places of great opportunity for flora and fauna, transitional spaces where organisms can take advantage of the opportunities of more than one habitat, often more than doubling their chances of finding food.

The word *ecotone* is a combination of the word *ecology*, the study of how humans and other organisms interact with their physical environment, and the Greek *tonos,* meaning *tension.* It makes sense. Anywhere different societies interact or integrate or overlap, there will be friction. We might remember that these frictions aren't inherently *bad,* even when they throw us for a loop. When we encounter something (or someone) new, we have the opportunity to gently reexamine our own assumptions and ways of being as we seek to learn from what (or whom) we've discovered. It is a chance to uncover additional possibilities. Ecotones are often tremendously lush and verdant places, after all. Life flourishes in diverse spaces that are rife with change; *we* can too.

When faced with liminal, transitional encounters in our own lives, whether we're entering a new community for the first time, beginning a burgeoning relationship, or integrating novel ways of being with our former ones, we have a choice to make. We can approach these challenges with a fight-or-flight, fawn-or-freeze response, as animals sometimes do, or we can take another cue from the natural world and meet them instead with curiosity.

Back in the 1960s, two researchers named Stephen Glickman and Richard Sores set out to study curiosity in zoo animals. They watched two hundred different species, putting novel objects into their enclosures and then observing how each individual animal responded. Primates showed the most consistent and sustained curiosity, which we might expect. But then the study got interesting. Predators like lions and tigers showed initial curiosity, but lost interest quickly. Rats mostly chewed on things. Adolescent animals tended to exhibit more curiosity than adults.

This study's findings on curiosity have been echoed in countless others since about animals and play. Playfulness is inherently a pursuit of curiosity, after all. *Let me try something! Ooh, that was interesting!* The more intelligent an animal is, the more it plays. Dolphins and apes and otters play quite a bit, for example, while insects and reptiles don't play at all. Intellectually advanced animals, including humans, begin much of their learning through play.

What happens when I do this? a baby wonders, tossing her rattle onto the floor. When a parent picks it up and returns it—hooray! She will throw it on the floor again with a smile, realizing she's stumbled onto a delightful game. She's also learning about gravity, cause and effect, and building relational connections, of course, but the motivation for continuing is that it's proving to be good fun.

Many animals practice curiosity and engage in play as a way to build skills too. They're constantly processing information about the world—what is good to eat, where predators may lurk, what spot is the most comfortable and safe to use for bedding down each night. So when more advanced animals—those we've mentioned but also intelligent bird species like parrots and corvids, canines like wolves, coyotes, and foxes, and felines like mountain lions and cheetahs—exhibit curiosity, the reason is often twofold. First, the world is an interesting place, and exploring it is fun. And second, any information they learn will likely be of use to them later, even if it isn't essential in the moment.

I once watched one of our neighborhood crows pull a diaper out of a neighbor's trash can. The rest of the flock gathered to investigate this new prize. The first pecked and poked at it, turning it over and over until its Velcro tabs gave way, spilling its contents onto the street, at which point every single crow hopped back in unison as if they'd been given an electric shock.

"This is *not* food," their joint recoil seemed to signal. "Lesson learned!" One by one they lifted off, flying across the cul-de-sac without any trace of chagrin. Animals don't berate themselves for discovering things the hard way. They don't apologize for their curiosity. After all, any bit of learning might one day be a useful one.

We often face the equivalent of ecotones in our own lives during times of change. One season blends into another. Someone new enters the family or the church or the office. Old patterns transition as a child is born or graduates, a parent newly requires care, we switch jobs. Perhaps we move to a new home or fall in love. We might pick up a new hobby, spending hours at the local bird marsh (ahem, *hypothetically*), as the rest of life shifts to accommodate our delight. (Sorry about missing dinner, Daryl!)

The natural world teaches us that an ocean is not its shore, and yet that shoreline will shift and change with the pull of the ocean's tides and storms. Ecotones are flux and integration, overlap and blend. They can come as a great relief—after hundreds of miles of desert, an oasis, or after countless rocky peaks, a verdant savanna. So often we think we want sameness and predictability when really the beauty is found in the challenging difference, the coming together, the merging of this and that.

A couple of years ago, two different worshiping communities approached our church leadership to ask about renting meeting space. After long conversations it was determined that both our life and theirs would be stretched and improved by not just sharing space but by combining elements of our ministries as well. Today a Mandarin-speaking Chinese church worships in one of our rooms on Sunday mornings, sending its children to our Sunday school programs and its teens to our small groups. We are always invited to join them for their post-worship meals. On Sunday afternoons, an Arabic fellowship meets downstairs for worship and encouragement, and its pastor, a man of deep wisdom and kindness, has guest preached in our services.

Our differences continue to matter—particularly the ways each community can hear the Word of God in the language it best understands—but the blending of our congregation with these newcomers and their groups with ours has been a deep blessing too. Ecotones allow two habitats to remain distinct while offering a nourishing, fruitful overlap.

"I made a new friend," my daughter Felicity, then five years old, told me, twirling her way out of Sunday school one morning early in these partnerships. "We don't always know each other's words, but we smiled a lot and played together."

"That's great, hon!" I said, juggling an armful of her artwork as we walked down the steps to hunt for more donuts. "What's her name?"

"Joy," she said. "Which makes sense." It did indeed.

Ecotones are rich with their intermixing of diverse plant and animal life, but they can also be particularly dangerous spaces. Predators love an ecotone, with its opportunities to collect prey from more than one habitat. Owls, eagles, and hawks wait at the tree line between forest and prairie or desert and highway knowing that rodents and birds and rabbits commonly traverse between the two. If the ecotone is where the prey's food is, their preferred insects or seeds or fruits or nectar, you can bet it is where the predator will lie in wait, as well.

We feel this, don't we? Transitional spaces are rarely restful ones. No one wants to permanently reside in an airport or a bus terminal. Expats long to hear hymns in their native language, to order breakfast without the hard work of translation. Our bodies sense that we are in more danger when traveling than safe at home. Transitions take us out of our comfort zones; change can put us on high alert.

But even when we are home, change can be perilous. Did you know that the highest time for at-home injuries is when people are decorating for the holidays? No one falls off a ladder because they're putting up twinkle lights for Ordinary Time. (Speaking of which, an average of thirty people each Christmas Day end up in the emergency room because of injuries sustained while *unwrapping gifts*. Easy there, tiger.)

Yet it is experiencing these transitions, letting them influence and shape us, not shying away from the tenuousness of the in-between times that allows us to participate in the fullness of the human experience. As John O'Donohue writes in *Anam Cara*, "The human journey is a continuous act of transfiguration." When we begin to approach these transitional times and spaces with curiosity rather than defensiveness, fear, assumptions, or judgment, we may begin to discover that there is goodness to be enjoyed wherever we are, whatever we face, and no matter where we end up.

Hebrews 11 is a wonderful study of faithfulness, but also a chronicle of transitions. *By faith* the universe was formed, going from formless and void to created and habituated. *By faith* Noah built an ark and then the rains began to fall. *By faith* Moses left Egypt, taking hundreds of thousands of people with him through the Red Sea on dry land. *By faith* Rahab hid the spies, and when her city fell, she was saved.

On the cusp of change, the edge of unfamiliarity, every person listed had the chance to flee or fight, freeze or fawn, yet each one chose the fifth option: faith. I used to think faith was a sort of blind belief, one where you had to put away your understanding of science or experience and just swallow it whole. But the more time I spend seeking Jesus, the more I've begun to realize that faith is really a sort of divine curiosity. The kind that is willing to step out on a limb with him. It's living into a holy question: *What if what God says is true?*

As Noah built a giant boat under a cloudless sky and Moses led hordes of formerly enslaved people out of Egypt and Rahab tied a red cord to her window, I can't imagine that they were certain. It is hard to be certain of anything when we are on the brink of disaster, poised on the precarious pinnacle between ruin and salvation. It is only in hindsight that all becomes clear. After the dove returns with an olive branch, when Moses can finally oversee the Promised Land, and at the moment Rahab and her family safely flee the ruins of Jericho, finding themselves welcomed into the Israelite camp, it is only then that truth solidifies into something weighty and fixed and knowable. *Look what God has done.* This helps us prepare for whatever is next with the same trusting curiosity: *Let's see what God will do next.*

When faced with change we often want answers and clarity and assurance. I know I do. Yet what God offers most often is not a map but a promise.

"Behold, I am with you always."

And somehow, this might be just enough.

7

Aging

The only constant is change.

HERACLITUS

ONE SUMMER IN MY LATE TEENS, I discovered a baby robin on the ground, barely feathered, shivering and alone. When I picked it up and cradled it in my hand, I could feel its frantic heart beating through the thin skin of its breast. Its pinfeathers were fluffed up at its temples like an eccentric professor, its mouth turned down in the typical robin scowl.

For most of a day I tried to feed it—worms, seeds, berries. I offered it a shallow dish of water and built it a nest of sticks and blanket scraps. I wasn't a birder yet, and the internet was still in its infancy. All I had to go on was my own untrained instinct and love of nature. But despite my best, bumbling efforts, the robin never ate or drank or made any sound at all. It just stared at me out of its glossy black eyes. I felt mute, helpless within its gaze. Finally, I did what I should have done in the first place—I called our local wildlife rehabilitation facility.

"How feathered is it?" they asked. "How big?" I described the bird—its brownish-gray plumage, its tiny, clawed feet, the way it fit in the palm of my hand.

"Likely newly fledged," they said. "Best put it back where you found it." Fledglings that leave the nest a bit too early often have a parent standing by, helping to feed and protect and guide them. Still, the brutal truth is that the majority of nestlings don't survive. Only about 25 percent of songbirds make it through their first year, and those that do have just a 50 percent chance of surviving the next one. Most birds never make it to full maturity.

I'm glad that I didn't know any of these statistics then, as I dutifully took the robin back into the fern-studded bracken of our side yard where I'd found it. There were foxes and fishers in the woods. Our neighbors all had dogs. But I didn't know what else to do.

Some birds take practice flights before officially leaving the nest. Great Blue Herons nest in trees—surprisingly, given their size and their love of the water—and will take many short warm-up jaunts, testing their gangly wings and learning how to land. Often a younger nestling, one that hatched a day or so later will watch these first few flights with keen interest. The last time I watched one test its wings, I could almost hear its sibling whisper, *"Dude!"*

One thing is certain: While leaving the nest is a hazardous endeavor, a nestling that refuses to leave its cozy home will also not survive. There is no growth without change, no passage to adulthood without leaving the nest, no aging well without courage. Just because a transition is frightening doesn't mean we can exempt ourselves. And holy curiosity can help give us the peace we need to take the leap.

"Getting old is the pits," my 103-year-old great-grandmother, Gramie B, would tell me, pulling her flowered, satin housecoat around her shoulders. After she turned ninety, she only got out of her pajamas to go to church or the casino. Respect.

It is one thing to practice curiosity when it comes to change that we have chosen: moving to a new place, initiating a shift in relationship, enrolling in a class. But much change comes to us in packages we didn't select and at times we don't prefer. A great deal of change simply happens to us: unchosen, unplanned, and often undesired. One of the steepest changes of this kind, inevitable and largely unwelcome, is that of aging.

The changes aging brings to us are frequently obnoxious. Many feel thrust upon us by malevolent forces—the wavering eyesight, the dad bod, the menopause belly, the hearing loss, the hair loss, the achy joints. Yesterday we were in our prime and now, today we have to hold a text message at arms' length in order to read it. We smile at the cute barista looking our way only to realize he is smiling at the twenty-something *behind* us. Leak proof undies are just around the corner. It's all so undignified. And so strangely unexpected.

"I'm fine getting old," I tell my friend Sonia, "I just didn't expect it to start so soon!" Aging is obvious and inevitable, yet it still manages to take so many of us by surprise. Who knew it would happen to *us*?

"Who is that old lady?" Gramie B would ask, pausing before the mirror in our hallway, putting a hand up to her soft, wrinkled cheek. "I do not feel like this on the inside."

Perhaps that sums up the most painful part of growing old—not the body, but the spirit. Our souls are eternally twenty-five, comfortably in our prime, yet our bodies, as the apostle Paul writes, are *wasting away*. No wonder there are billion-dollar industries dedicated to maintaining the illusion of youth—long, thick hair; strong, white teeth; clear, wide eyes; smooth, taut skin. Is it so wrong to want to look the way we feel on the inside? (On the inside I have six-pack abs, by the way.)

Hannah Arendt once wrote to a friend that the most difficult part of aging was its "relentless defoliation." She was not bothered by her own physical changes but rather the "transformation of a world with familiar faces (no matter, foe or friend) into a kind of desert, populated by strange faces. In other words, it is not me who withdraws but the world that dissolves—an altogether different proposition." Arendt describes the universal truth that the older we get, the more likely the landscape around us is to have become alien and unfamiliar. Technology outpaces us, empires rise and fall, and one day we look out over our hometown or congregation or workplace and realize we don't recognize it anymore at all. Daryl and I recently attended our twentieth college reunion, and truthfully, we may never be the same again, haunted as we are by the changes two decades have wrought on us all and the mirror that reunion held up to us both.

As the years spin beneath my own wheels, I better understand why so many of us become harder and more bitter as the decades go on. Aches and pains are no small things to live with. In his "Lines on Retirement after Reading Lear," the poet David Wright warns his readers to fend off the dangers of getting older:

> Avoid storms. And retirement parties.
> You can't trust the sweetnesses your friends will
> offer, when they really want your office,
> which they'll redecorate.

The world changes so quickly that it becomes difficult to keep up. Our bodies seem to turn on us. Friends and loved ones abandon us in death, one after the other, leaving the world a lonelier, more unfriendly place.

Yet I've seen the changes of aging turn people kinder too. Some of the best folks I know have suffered tremendously, but the hard changes they have experienced seem to have sanded down their rough edges rather than turn them brittle and bereaved. They'd grown deep roots during easier, simpler seasons, connecting themselves to the source of all life. As the psalmist writes, the one who delights in the Lord is *like a tree planted by streams of water . . . whose leaf does not wither*. When the storms of change and the anguishes of aging came, they approached them with curiosity. Humility. Grace.

"God has been so kind to me," a mentor once told me, his body racked with Parkinson's. "God has been so, so kind."

Faced with the reality that our bodies will decay, that our minds will lose their sharpness, that we will bury friends and coworkers and even spouses, and that eventually we will all ourselves succumb to death, the temptation is to ignore, deny, or distract ourselves away from this pain. But perhaps, instead, we might embrace aging with gentleness, as kind to ourselves as we would be to a dear friend.

As I step into my mid-forties and beyond, walking alongside people in their eighties and beyond, I have hopes and plans to emulate the best of them. I want to prepare now for what will be inevitable. I want to join those who accept their new limitations while seeking to live faithfully with the time they have left. Those who stay curious: packing our local community college's free emeritus classes to learn watercolor painting or birding (yes!) or new technology. Those who receive babies at the church nursery on Sundays and lead groups on grief and memoir and cancer support. Those who meet me at the church door with a word of wisdom, encouragement, reminder, or cheer.

Though I have an innate allergy to Proverbs 31 after all the ways I've seen and experienced its weaponization against women (not to mention the times it is read as "for wives only," leaving out whole vast swaths of faithful single women and all men!), but when it is read through the lens of aging, the passage sparks back to life:

She is clothed with strength and dignity, it reads. *She can laugh at the days to come.*

You won't see many old animals in the wild. Creatures that slow down with the passing of years become easy prey, and even apex predators decline quickly when they can no longer chase after antelope or snatch salmon from a stream. It is tricky to measure the lifespan of certain species out in nature, as it can be near-impossible to follow a rare or reclusive animal all the way from birth (or hatching!) to death. Many of our best guesses come from animals born in zoos or on wildlife preserves, but because predation is much less common there, it skews our studies. Yet we can tell from basic scientific observation that the earth is not always kind to older, weaker creatures.

This is true of our American culture as well. The elderly are not revered or respected as they are in many other parts of the world. Caregiving is often viewed as a burden; most older people will die in nursing homes, hospitals, or other facilities, not in a family home. We hide, ignore, and even ridicule those nearing the end of life. No wonder we want to run from aging when it comes to our own bodies.

Yet growing older is a unique opportunity to embrace the profound, beautiful, and difficult gifts of this particular type of change. It can put us in touch with the truth of our mortality, a truth that is perhaps uncomfortable but also, in a strange and holy way, *good*. Wright's poem continues:

> In the end, no one leaves
> the stage in character—we never see
> the feather, the mirror held to our lips.

This is what the church seeks to remind us of on Ash Wednesday: That we are mortal and our days on this earth are not infinite. We come from the dust, and to the dust we will return. It is sad and tragic—and weirdly encouraging too. There is relief in naming things as they are, in probing them with curiosity, in embracing what is real.

"Remember you are dust," I say to one congregant after another, my fingers and their foreheads smeared with ashes, a biblical sign of mourning. A sign of death. While our culture encourages us to despise aging and seek after the impossibility of eternal youth—attempting to persuade us that perhaps with just a little bit more money or hair dye or ab work, we, too, could be immortal—Scripture testifies to the deep truth that we are finite creatures who will one day grow old.

This is the case not only for us but for the whole of our universe as well. Both Isaiah and Hebrews tell us that the earth will *wear out like a garment*. It is fearful to think of our only home growing threadbare, our planet developing rips and tears. And certainly there is much more climate stewardship that needs to be done. (More on that in chapter eleven.) For now, just the short answer: we need not fear, for this is not the story's end. God's salvation—of us and of the earth we love and depend on—*will last forever*.

I'd never heard the word before the doctor uttered it. She did so casually, an offhanded remark in the midst of our usual litany of questions and answers. Any significant changes to my diet? No. Any concerns about my skin or overall health? No. How were my periods? Well, they had become quite a bit heavier than normal, and my cycle had recently changed from the thirty-two-day rhythm I'd had for my entire adult life to a much shorter twenty-six-day one.

"Oh, you've likely started perimenopause," she said.

"But I'm not fifty!" I said, laughing, trying to put a pleasant spin on my annoyance that the person holding my medical chart had suddenly added a decade to my age.

"Menopause happens around fifty," she said. "That's when you haven't had a period for a full year. Perimenopause takes place continually for roughly a decade beforehand." I had no follow-up questions until the shock wore off a few hours later at home, at which point I commenced researching. Reading article after article, one grumpy phrase kept rattling around in my mind: *I did not sign up for this.* But perimenopause, it turned out, was my new reality.

In general, I like to think that I've made my peace with getting older. In Southern California, the land of plastic surgery, beach bodies, and perpetual youth, I view aging naturally and gracefully as part of my ministry. I want to go to my grave with all of my original parts and few additives, if I can help it. Aging isn't something I dread or fear. Yet I would have preferred to be at least a little bit prepared before this new hormonal wave took the reins of my good humor and my sanity. It felt like someone had performed a bait-and-switch with my plans for the entire next decade. The whole situation reminded me of the kindly nurse who walked into my hospital room after the birth of our first baby.

"These are for you!" she said, her voice a Wisconsin lilt. She handed me a cellophane-wrapped package. "Your mesh undies!"

"My mesh *what now*?" I asked, downing a couple of ibuprofen and rubbing my bleary eyes.

"Well, you'll need them to hold those big pads for the postpartum bleeding."

"The *what*?"

"The postpartum bleeding. It's like a very heavy period. But don't worry, dear, it only goes on for about six weeks or so. If you pass any clots bigger than a golf ball, you go ahead and give us a call."

Now, faced with this recent perimenopausal revelation, this unwanted gift, I did what I always do in the face of incredulity—I checked out books on the subject. Their pages described nearly a dozen symptoms I'd deemed too mild to mention at a medical appointment but found significantly irritating nonetheless. Itchy skin. Disruptions in sleep. Random rage. Unexplained weight gain. During perimenopause, previously synched hormones become erratic, leading to huge peaks and valleys, sometimes within the same hour. Then there were the listed symptoms I had yet to experience but now could put on my internal List of Things to Dread: hot flashes, thinning hair, a loss of bone density so significant it could result in limb fractures from nothing more strenuous than standing up. And finally, there was the humiliating kicker for someone in her late thirties—acne.

A day or two later Daryl found me buried in research, a stack of pink books—*why* do publishers think women want pink books?—at my side.

"Daryl," I said. "This explains *so much.*"

What it didn't explain was how someone who faithfully went to her annual appointment every year, who read what could perhaps even be deemed *an unhealthy amount*, had never run across even the word *perimenopause* before. I knew more about prostate cancer than the phase of life I had entered, and I didn't have a single close friend or family member suffering from that. As Kenn Kaufman wisely notes in *The Birds Audubon Missed,* "Our perceptions are shaped by the names and definitions we apply to things." The birder in me knew that naming the reality was only one small step, but a very important one nevertheless. Putting words to things begins the process of demystification and—down the road—often acceptance too.

But I wasn't ready yet.

"I finally—*finally*—made peace with my body," I told Daryl. "After being pregnant and postpartum and nursing and then pregnant again for the entire past decade, I found an equilibrium and now I discover that everything is about to get tossed in the spin cycle again! Perimenopause feels very unfair."

"It is very unfair," Daryl agreed, his back toward me, rummaging in a kitchen cabinet. I knew what he was doing. I heard the electric kettle turn on and a few moments later he gently pushed a cup of tea toward me. I didn't need *comfort*; I wanted to *rage*. I took a sip. The warmth slid right down and started to spread its calm, darn it anyway.

A year or so after my college graduation, I met a favorite professor for lunch and lamented how hard the transition to post-college life was. I bemoaned my minimum-wage job and decrepit apartment and difficult roommates and surprising loneliness.

"No one told me it would be this hard," I said.

"If anyone had told you," he asked, not unkindly, "would you have been ready to hear it?"

Perhaps that was the real issue. While women's health research and care still aren't on par with that of men, once I started looking, information was everywhere, from *The New England Journal of Medicine* to Oprah's website. Instagram's algorithm quickly picked up on my nascent interest and began offering me ads for questionable weight-loss supplements and "miracle" wrinkle treatments. Maybe we see only what we're looking for. Maybe we prepare only for the transitions we want.

The next day, I commiserated with my friend Anna. Though she is a few years older than I am, it turned out that her journey into perimenopause started concurrently with mine. (This is another fun element of these hormonal changes—they start when they start, which can be anytime between a woman's late twenties and early fifties. How does a person prepare for *that*?)

"Will you send me a book recommendation?" she asked. "One of the good ones?" I nodded. We both tend to face our fears armed with the knowledge of experts. We like to gather information to find the best way through. We're also both Enneagram Threes, happiest when projects are completed, boxes ticked, plans confirmed, curveballs avoided.

"I think what's the most difficult for me is that this will be an ongoing thing for years and years and years," I said. "It feels a bit like an open wound. How can I find a way to be at peace amid constant change?"

"That's the question, isn't it?" she said. "That's the whole thing."

Practicing curiosity can help us grow in our tolerance for uncertainty, a vital part of aging well. In Christian circles we might even call uncertainty tolerance *trust.* As we read in the book of James, *Why, you do not even know what will happen tomorrow. What is your life? You are a mist that appears for a little while and then vanishes.* These strong statements are followed with a reminder of who is truly in control.

Instead, you ought to say, "If it is the Lord's will, we will live and do this or that." It is natural to want to see the full path set out before us. Yet God doesn't hand us a map of the entire journey. Instead we are invited to follow, practicing holy curiosity. To take the next single step of obedience, trusting that God will guide us in the one after that too. I love how Peter Harris puts it in his book, *Under the Bright Wings.* A British birder and cofounder of A Rocha, a Christian conservation ministry, Harris knows a thing or two about stepping out in faith. He writes, "The search to know the will of God may well begin with us wanting to find out more of the future, but it ends by our being drawn into relationship with the Father, and often thereby living comfortably with many uncertainties."

Aging is all about uncertainty. The majority of us will end up nursing injuries or ailments we never would have chosen. Very few of us will know the number of our days. Yet God invites us into deeper relationship through these unpredictabilities. Like Moses and Miriam, we are called away from our familiar home, to follow God to the land that is promised. A land we've never seen but are nevertheless asked to trust will be ready and waiting for us.

The hope of weathering change is not that we would never *weather*. Even the flintiest of rocks will wear away with time. If we are blessed with years, we will each grow old. We will soften and bend. Our skin will mottle, and our hair will thin. Life will hand us humility. It will also grant wisdom, if we choose to receive it. Aging is not a change to fear or run from, but to acknowledge, accept, and expect.

The God who is beyond and outside of time promises to see us through.

8

Flocking

That's the real problem.
We don't even think of ducks as musicians.

TED FLOYD

FOR THE AVERAGE NON-BIRDER, a duck is a Mallard. These familiar birds, memorialized in children's books like *Make Way for Ducklings,* have become, for most, not only the gold standard but the only duck out there. We see them at lakes and parks and ponds. We can easily picture the males with their iridescent emerald heads, the females streaked brown and cream with one shiny patch of royal blue on their wings. Or perhaps we have seen domestic ducks on a farm, fat-bottomed and white-feathered, gobbling grain and giving new meaning to the word *waddle.* But that's it. A duck is a duck is a duck.

What if I told you there were forty-four species of duck native to North America and an estimated 150 worldwide? This number doesn't even include swans, geese, or other waterfowl like herons and egrets! Mallards are just the tip of the delightfully ducky iceberg. There are *so* many different ducks to discover.

The biodiversity within their family astonishes. There are dabbling ducks and perching ducks, diving ducks and domestic ducks. There are also sea ducks—those who spend much or sometimes even all of their lives on the open ocean. (Some ornithologists put sea ducks in a separate category than other North American ducks, but for our purposes, particularly because both are called ducks, let's keep them together.) Dabbling ducks do just what their family name suggests: they dabble. Straining their food from lakes and ponds, they dip their heads, pull up a mouthful, and sieve out the water. These ducks like to float upon the surface and then tip forward—duck butt alert!—to fish their food from the shallows. Diving ducks duck all the way under the water for their food. Perching ducks make their homes up in trees, a startling sight to anyone who didn't know that ducks can do that.

I once spent a morning in a forest preserve in Grand Rapids. A quarter mile down the trail, I spotted an unusual bird poking its head in and out of a tree cavity. It was too big to be a woodpecker and its beak was too thick. Plus, it looked like it was wearing a sort of Star Wars Rebel Fleet-style helmet, but green. I took a side trail until I could get close enough to make a positive identification—it was a Wood Duck drake! The first perching duck that I'd seen actually aloft. As I waited, the hen eventually peeked out too.

This is one of the wonders of birding—to almost every rule there is an exception. To nearly every established norm, there is an outlier or two. Ducks nest on the ground. Except, of course, for the ones that don't.

Domestic ducks have been bred and cross-bred in captivity, and their numbers and variants are usually not included when we are speaking of native North American ducks (much like a Labrador retriever wouldn't be counted in a local coyote census). Still, they're a wonder on their own, and they often wing their way over to local lakes and ponds and mix with wild ducks.

Ducks are remarkably sociable and flexible, practicing a wide welcome to other duck species and often even interbreeding, creating new duck hybrids. It is not uncommon to see a mixed flock of ducks living in harmony—Northern Shovelers and Cinnamon Teal and Mallards, for example. Scanning a seemingly uniform group huddled on a shore or floating in a lake can lead to a delightful lightbulb moment—that Common Goldeneye among all the other Common Goldeneye is actually a Barrow's! It can also be a bit maddening to try to pick out who is who in a mixed flock, particularly when females of different species can look very similar. But the mingling is good for the ducks, who find safety and comfort in numbers.

It helps that ducks as a whole tend to be a placid, gentle sort. They aren't particularly territorial or vocal, and as long as newcomers give them respectful space and don't pester their young, they are likely to be accepted. Ducks are the welcoming committee of the bird world, the ones who would staff the visitor center at the national park.

"We're glad you're here," they might say. "Now remember to pack out your trash and don't start any fires."

Ducks illustrate aspects of a healthy congregation, all swimming in the same direction but in a variety of different expressions. If a church is all one age group or race or socioeconomic status it can quickly become an echo chamber rather than a vibrant worshiping body. Variations in gifting, strength, and life experience serve to enhance a community, to strengthen it.

This isn't to say that bringing together a diverse body of believers is easy. In *Life Together,* Dietrich Bonhoeffer wrote of the pain—and thus importance—of Christian community. He contrasts Christian idealism, the false belief that we can create a perfect, easy society, with the gritty reality that living and worshiping together will always involve a bit of conflict. "The person who loves their dream of a Christian community more than the Christian community itself become destroyers of that Christian community," he wrote. But the person who loves those around them with the help of Jesus, different and complex as those other people might be, can create real, lasting community.

It is this challenge to which Christ calls each of us. These waterfowl teach us that differences need not be a threat; that change is not the enemy.

Perhaps both might even be a strength.

It's midsummer and the Argentine ants are back, snaking their way in orderly lines through the infinitesimally small cracks between our window and door seals. Smaller than an eighth of an inch, these little pests plague the homes of Southern California residents at this time of year, when the heat turns from toasty to downright oppressive.

During my childhood summers in Wisconsin we faced pavement ants that would find their way inside searching for sugar and crumbs. But the Argentine ants don't want food from our home—they're on the hunt for water. I lay on my stomach and watch them march from the patio door across the floor of the playroom, undeterred by the few fluffy kernels of popcorn hiding beneath our coffee table. They keep to the grooves in the floorboards, a type of camouflage shielding them from obvious perception. They are headed for the kitchen sink, where the water is. They made this trek last year, too, and somehow they've remembered the path.

Ants don't come in flocks, of course. Their collective noun is *colony*, a word with a decidedly invading tinge. To be a colonizer is not friendly to those already living in the place that will be overtaken. Yet Argentine ants display qualities we find in our friends the ducks: teamwork, collectivity, peacefulness, cooperation. In southern Europe, these insects have been observed forming "supercolonies," massive collections of ants that are able to coexist well due to their lack of aggression toward one another. The authors of one study note, "Some ants have an extraordinary social organization, called unicoloniality, whereby individuals mix freely among physically separated nests." This curious behavior is quite unusual among ants, the majority of which have evolved to recognize their own in-group and keep the out groups—even if they are the same species—*out*.

Other species take these divisions to the extreme. *Colobopsis saundersi*, often referred to as the Malaysian exploding ant or even the suicide ant, will fiercely defend its own in-group. According to entomologists, "during territorial combat, workers of some species sacrifice themselves by rupturing their gaster and releasing sticky and irritant contents of their . . . gland reservoirs to kill or repel rivals." The gaster is the enlarged part of an ant's abdomen—the third part of an ant's three segments, located behind its head and thorax. While there are over twelve thousand known species of ants on earth, luckily for the rest of the insect world, only fifteen of these are known to explode.

But back to our Argentine ant friends. They are still marching, marching, marching into our house, seeking hydration. Seeking survival. Argentine ants thrive in both rural and urban environments because of their resourcefulness. Poor diggers, they nest shallowly in sandy soil, the cracks of foundations or sidewalks, and under leaf litter. If another ant colony vacates a well-dug burrow, Argentines will quickly and happily fill it. They work cooperatively to find food, move eggs, and protect their queen, all while refusing to pick fights with other insects whenever they can help it. These qualities have helped them become established from their original habitat in northern Argentina, Uruguay, Bolivia, Paraguay, and eastern Brazil to their now worldwide spread from Australia to South Africa to Europe and southern North America. They now rank on the list of top one hundred worst invasive animal species—a feat, knowing that the list also includes the common malaria mosquito. We've been colonized, but by such a placid, friendly insect type. Pest species or no, we can learn quite a bit from them about strength in numbers and how to adapt to new locations by working together to make a home.

They'd almost be cute, if they weren't taking over my kitchen sink.

The church I pastor today is not primarily red or blue, Republican or Democrat, though we have people who lean hard politically to both the left and the right. There are a good number of centrists in our midst, too, as well as the politically fed up. Still, we strive to find our unity in Christ, in paddling in the same direction toward the one who gives us life. Our diversity strengthens us rather than divides, though this often requires the practice of challenging Christian virtues like forbearance and patience. Nurturing it requires us to practice a healthy theology of change: everything from preparation to curiosity, adaptability to resilience. Curiosity in particular has become, for us, a spiritual discipline.

We don't always nail it. We stumble about as often as we succeed. But there is grace even in the attempt. The apology after a misstep provides the opportunity to build new bridges, to form deeper bonds. And God graciously brings us, time and time again, to the realization that we aren't home yet; that we all still have much to learn.

I'll never forget a Presbytery meeting from years back that centered on radical welcome. We talked about how we could include those who were often unintentionally excluded from worship: the hard of hearing, the visually impaired, those whose primary language wasn't English. At the end we were invited to stand in a circle around the spacious chancel in order to receive the Lord's Supper together. The bread would be passed and then the cup.

"Is there a gluten-free option?" I whispered to one of the hosts. I'm one of a handful of severely gluten intolerant members of our Presbytery, and the team is usually good about offering us safe meals and snacks. But before I'd even finished my sentence, the host's face paled.

"Oh no," she said. "I'm really sorry." It wasn't a deep wound—I often visit churches where I am inadvertently left out of the sacrament. Many parishes are small, others believe that no one in their midst is in need of these types of elements. In fact, when I first began ministry at my current church in California, our elders suspected the same. It was awkward for me to ask for accommodations, especially as the only one we knew of who needed them. Yet when we began offering gluten-free Communion, more than half a dozen men and women came to me privately to say thanks.

"I haven't taken Communion for years," one told me. "I just didn't want to be a bother." What is Christian love other than the willingness to be "bothered"? To love a brother or sister deeply enough that their request becomes not a burden but an honor? A joy? To seek, as Saint Francis once wisely instructed, first to understand, not just to be understood? When a few of our political centrists expressed their discomfort to a man who commonly wore his red MAGA hat to worship, he left it at home. When we remodeled one of our worship spaces that had stairs to reach the chancel, we put in a ramp. The very week it was completed, a woman in a wheelchair pulled up to me in worship and gasped.

"There's a ramp," she said, putting a hand on my arm. "Thank you."

We still have miles to go, of course. I have just as many gaps in knowledge and patience as the next person—too eager for expediency, sometimes at the expense of another's unspoken needs. But God is good: New neighbors continue to arrive to teach us how to listen, to ask the right questions, to stay curious about what new changes God may be calling us to make. These friends teach us anew how to bend in the way of Christ, the suffering servant who kneels to wash our feet.

This flexibility does not mean we call sin holiness or leave all worship structure behind. Wisdom will be required as we learn when and how far to flex and when to hold firm. "All people are welcome," my pastor-friend Anna is fond of saying, "but not all behaviors are welcome." Biblical teaching, good order, and theological depth are important, after all. A church is a church, not a political rally or a dance party or a free for all.

A healthy tree will stand strong in the wind. It will bend but not break. But a wet noodle won't stand at all. As a leadership coach I know likes to say when he's tried to assist someone who has no interest in growth: You can't push a rope.

A group of ducks is called a *raft*, a *team*, or a *paddling*. Even their collective nouns nod to the group, to strength found in numbers. Ducks intuitively understand that we weather change better together, even though some feathers will inevitably get ruffled along the way.

One of my earliest ministry mentors told me often not to isolate. He'd seen my introversion and how prone I was to over-function. Why ask for help if I could just do things myself? After a pastoral sabbatical in 2022, when Jesus, friends, and therapists helped pull me back from the brink of burnout, I was determined to return to ministry in a different way. No longer would pastoring be primarily a solo project where I took all of the matters entrusted to me into my own hands. I wanted to learn to be a duck, not a raven, to lead and handle change collaboratively instead of all on my own.

This was—is—an uphill climb. I *am* prone to isolating. I come from a long line of hermit-adjacent folks, after all. Near the end of his life, my grandfather rarely even left his house except to go down to the lake just beyond and watch the wildlife. Going it alone is in my DNA. But there are times that each of us needs to flex against our natural way of bending, to grow new muscles and develop new skills. To *change*.

When transitions come to church or home, when Daryl and I face something new with the kids or within our marriage, we are learning to look to our flock. There is not only safety in numbers but wisdom too. Help and kindness and care, listening ears or a meal or a ride or an hour without our kids so that we can take time to work out a problem we've been too busy to address.

Being more like the ducks and the ants will require flexibility. Bearing with. It will mean not only receiving help and care but taking the time to offer it too. But if I've learned anything as I approach life's halfway mark, with many changes yet to weather, it's that being part of a flock is a gift well worth accepting.

9

Migration

I could not help it:
the restlessness was in my nature;
it agitated me to pain sometimes.

CHARLOTTE BRONTË

A COUPLE OF YEARS AGO, I noticed one morning that a Black-headed Grosbeak had popped up at our birdbath, seemingly by magic. The day before, the yard was all finches and hummingbirds, but now this handsome creature with its namesake black head, thick bill, orange body, and bright white wing patches was splashing about as though it owned the place. The next day, it was gone.

Researching the science behind where these surprise birds came from felt like uncovering a cosmic secret. It turns out that most songbirds migrate in the dead of night. But as Kenn Kaufman notes, "They will go unnoticed except by the birders out looking for them." This profound miracle happens largely unobserved.

I've talked to more than one ornithologist, scientists to the core, who admit that migration is basically an enchantment of sorts. No one knows how it works, how fledglings have destinations written into the hollow of their bones, how birds navigate in near-pitch-blackness on moonless nights, or why the tremendous outlay of energy is worth it, particularly for birds who migrate to places with similar climates or food sources to the ones they leave behind.

But every spring and fall millions of birds discern that it's time to leave and then they make their way overhead under blackened, starry heavens, headed to new destinations or more likely, the same ones their parents traveled to, and their parents' parents before them. While you prepare for bed, scrolling on your phone or brushing your teeth or enjoying spring's first warm evening breeze from the window, overhead are grosbeaks and buntings and sparrows and tanagers and warblers already on their way flying, flying, flying.

Passerines undertake their migratory journeys at night for several reasons—fewer predators, less fluctuation in temperature, cooler skies. On nights when the stars are out, they find their way home with an eye to the midnight skies like ancient seafarers on inky seas. What amazes me the most is that birds that have never migrated before, hatched and grown and newly fledged from their nests, somehow find their way, too, many without flocks to guide them.

"It's magic," I say when I talk to naturalists and biologists and birding scientists of all stripes.

"It is," they tell me. "It really is."

Fresh out of seminary, I relished the opportunity to wear many ministry hats at my first pastorate in Wisconsin, to test my skills and try my theories, preaching and teaching and moderating our church board meetings, but also sitting in the stands at high school football games and stacking cans in the food pantry and shoveling the snowy path leading to the sanctuary when the plow ran late. As the only woman among the area's seven ministers—with a church on every corner, our little town represented a good array of denominations—I found myself pleasantly surprised when the men received me warmly as one of their own.

When Daryl and I welcomed our first baby, a sweet boy named Lincoln who was born with a perpetually furrowed brow and an absolute aversion to sleep, I holed up for a quick six weeks of parental leave. Like most first-time moms, I intended to bounce right back. But

I soon discovered it was less of a bounce and more of a crawl. Our new son refused every bottle of pumped milk Daryl offered him, leaving me as his sole source of nourishment as he woke four, five, *six* times each night. My long pastoral hours and gaps in experience, especially when combined with the rigors of new parenting far from the support of extended family, began to take a toll.

"This may not be sustainable," I commented, feeding Lincoln while checking my watch. I'd left a funeral supper mid-main course in the church basement and needed to be back by dessert.

As Daryl and I pondered and prayed over the trajectory of our lives and ministries, we both felt restless. Behind each of our conversations was the flickering sense that God might be calling us somewhere new. But still, I didn't want to leave. I couldn't *imagine* leaving. I loved and trusted this congregation. They loved and trusted me. I was as green as they come and stumbled into completely avoidable mistakes more often than I'd like to admit. But the congregation was enjoying stability for the first time in many years, a full-time minister dedicated to their common work. They'd stretched to afford a pastoral salary, but now our budget was in the black, the pews filled, the gardens weeded, and the committees healthy. Each of these successes had been a big lift for all of us. We were proud of what we'd built together.

But when the Spirit of God starts brooding over the waters, waking us up in the middle of the night, stirring our hearts to something new, change can be very hard to withstand.

"I found a church we might want to look at," Daryl said one day, handing his closed laptop to me as we sat down to dinner one Saturday evening. From our dining room window, I could see the lights on in the sanctuary, the custodian finishing her vacuuming of its red carpets and pews before the next morning's worship. She had become a friend, at first uncomfortable with the idea of a woman minister—she worshiped with the Baptists down the road—but slowly warming to me as we spent hours together in the quiet church. It turned out that we had a lot in common. It turned out that, for a lady pastor, I wasn't very scary after all. She'd recently told me that she was expecting a baby of her own in just a few months. How could I leave her? How could I leave any of them?

"I don't really want to look," I told Daryl.

"I know," he said. "And you don't have to unless you want to." We locked eyes. Approaching change with curiosity is key for weathering it well, but we aren't always ready to be curious. Sometimes we need to warm up to a new idea, to let it marinate and simmer until the time is right. Curiosity cannot be forced, but only invited.

I set the computer aside.

"Maybe after dinner."

There is a German word for the unsettledness birds display as they prepare to migrate. *Zugunruhe* comes from two words, the first meaning *migration* and the second, *restlessness*. In the weeks and days preceding their long flights, birds often become agitated. It is not yet time for them to go, but they feel a yearning in their bodies, a magnetic pull to somewhere else. Somewhere new. They display great patience during this disquiet. It is the start of their migratory preparation, but they know not to go too soon. To migrate successfully, temperatures, timing, and weather all need to cooperate. Food sources not only at their destination but at their travel stops along the way must be re-established from their winter lulls.

It's a precarious undertaking, migration, yet birds are compelled to rise to the challenge year after year—and not just once, but *twice* annually. And in this desire to *go*, to *move*, to travel hundreds or even thousands of miles, we discover that great effort can be a beautiful thing. Think of what a tern must encounter in her journey—icebergs and container ships, breeching whales and tropical breezes, polar bears in the north and penguins in the south. Wonders beyond wonder, and in such vast diversity and array. Though it is easier, almost always, to stay put, we will miss the breathtaking vistas if we never we take flight.

As birds' *Zugunruhe* increases, eventually it becomes impossible to withstand. Whatever instinctual magnetic pull sends birds up into the skies, risking all to make it a few dozen more miles north or south, it is not easy, but neither is it optional. They must go.

One of the most fascinating migrations on earth takes place twice annually, between April and June and then again between October and late November each year in the Sea of Cortez—also known as the Gulf of California—off the western coast of mainland Mexico. But this one doesn't involve birds. Our avian friends don't have a monopoly on the magic of migration.

Mobula Rays, sometimes called Devil Rays, thrive in warm waters. These massive sea creatures grow to seventeen feet in length and can weigh as much as a jeep. Mobulas can breach spectacularly, jumping up to six feet in the air. Though they are part of the broader species of rays that have venomous barbs in their tails, Mobulas themselves do not sting. They are whip smart, with one of the largest brain-to-body ratios of any fish. They can even pass the mirror test—a basic animal intelligence exam where scientists discern whether a species can recognize its own reflection. The rays are oviparous, meaning they produce eggs *internally,* then those eggs hatch *inside the mother,* so that they give birth to actual live young. Tens of thousands of Mobulas meet up in the Sea of Cortez in the late spring and early autumn each year, migrating from the open ocean to gather in massive, churning groups.

And here's the cool part: *We don't know why.* There are some theories, of course, but our knowledge of these massive, fantastic beasts is very minimal. For example, only one has ever been witnessed giving birth—and that was in an aquarium. There's no consensus on why they breach or migrate or gather in such large groups. Though there are tourist organizations taking people to see them, to swim or snorkel or dive with them, much of how they do what they do—not to mention *why*—is shrouded in mystery.

I cling to this wonder with a weird sort of hope. Every year tens of thousands of massive ocean beasts travel back to the Sea of Cortez. Their migratory pods have been featured in *Blue Planet* and *Nat Geo* specials. People flock to see them. The rays gather in the same locations year upon year. And then they disappear into the depths of the open ocean, taking all their mysteries with them.

So much of our lives are shrouded in unknowing. Not only our own futures, but also our motivations and needs and desires are often obscured to us. Why do we do what we do? How can we undertake our next steps with clarity and purpose? We move about at random or else with intention but in the wrong direction. We guess and second guess. We do our best and even then fall so very short of what we'd hoped for. What's next, and how might we best prepare for it? We often don't know. But here's the thing: *God always does.*

Because I know who holds the future, as the old hymn tells us. *Life is worth the living.* Someday we may untangle the mystery of where the Mobulas go. We may film them giving birth in the pitch-black deep. Surely there are marine biologists working out new discoveries about these rays even now. The mysteries invite us to explore them, to seek to understand.

Likewise, often on the other side of massive changes in our lives, we can look back and see—oh, *that's* why. But right now, today, if we are on the cusp of possible change, we can open our minds and hearts and hands and accept that something is unsettled within us, approaching our *Zugunruhe* with curiosity. It's often the first step in discovering what's next.

The restlessness itself can be a clue.

Not all birds migrate. Many stay put within the same few square miles for their entire lives. California's Channel Islands National Park boasts a singular species of jay—the Island Scrub Jay—that exists only on Santa Cruz Island, a rocky outcropping in the southeastern Pacific that's just ninety-six square miles and inhabited only by a handful of park rangers. Santa Cruz lies eight short miles from the mainland, across the deep, whale-frequented fissure of a channel that gives the island group its name. This distance would be no big deal for most songbirds, and a mere hop for a tern or a gull. But the Island Scrub Jay won't fly to the mainland. It simply does not migrate. These beautiful, scrappy birds have been stationed only on Santa Cruz Island for hundreds of years and, assuming conservation efforts to protect them continue, they will live there and only there for hundreds still to come.

I love the intransigent species, the American Crows and the California Quail, the Northern Cardinals and Spruce Grouse and Black-Capped Chickadees. They were born to stay put, to let their lives come and go in a single forest or park or neighborhood. They are hardy enough to weather seasonal changes and clever enough to find food amidst the blazes of summer and the chills of winter. Nature needs those of us who like to stay too.

But even those of us who'd prefer to remain sometimes don't have a choice. Circumstances lead us to the decision that change is necessary, a move is required by a job. Or the restlessness grows until it can no longer be ignored.

I loved pastoring in Wisconsin. It was knit into my soul—the people, the landscape, the weather, the culture. I loved our church; we were building something transcendent together there on the wind-swept Wisconsin farmlands.

But I was feeling the *Zugunruhe*.

How do we know when it is time for a change? So much change is simply thrust upon us, unchosen, that it can feel tricky to establish when we should *choose* a change that is within our decision-making power. Determining whether or not to pursue a change falls under the category of discernment: listening to the Lord, seeking wise council, and determining what such a change might mean for us and those we love. We might sit with a choice, a potential change, and weigh it in our souls.

In her beautiful book *The Understory,* Lore Wilbert, who graciously wrote the forward to this book (be still, my heart!), writes of learning to listen to her gut after years—decades—of being taught to distrust it: "God has not abdicated my innermost being. He has put down roots and abides there, and therefore my gut or intuition or sense or spirit *is* trustworthy, even if I don't know where I'm being led or if I'll get there in one piece." Discernment is an exercise in curiosity. It doesn't necessarily mean choosing the easy thing or the comfortable thing or that which makes our souls stand up and shout—though sometimes it does. God won't always lead us up the steepest, rockiest vistas. But sometimes, God will.

The decision to leave our beloved church in Wisconsin back in 2014 was a hard and painful one. Yet the discernment itself was not an unfamiliar task. Daryl and I had been there before with other major life choices. We'd weighed whether to marry and when, where to attend graduate school, when to pursue starting a family. Each time we'd been driven to our knees, to the hard work of prayerful introspection, and to seeking advice from those whose wisdom we respected most.

Together we would sit with what we'd learned, sifting it all through practices of prayer and curiosity, and then slowly but steadily, a strange peace would descend on us both. Not necessarily because the decision we'd arrived at was easy, but because we sensed the Lord's leading and equipping, the Spirit's presence preparing us for what was to come. These moments have felt to me like Frederick Buechner's writings about knowing that "all is right deep down."

He continues, describing the grace of "riding that trust the way a red-tailed hawk rides the currents of the air in this valley where we live."

Hawks migrate. Vast groups of them gather in swirling kettles, congregating upon rising thermals, soaring over ridges and across forests. No one really knows how they do it. No one but God. And this same God will walk beside us on our own journey of choices and changes, buoying us up. Helping us to see what comes next.

Adaptation:

| the ability to learn something new in one circumstance and then apply that learning elsewhere.

Adaptation enables us to learn new skills while setting aside those that no longer serve us. Think of a hungry crow that can't reach the ants deep in an anthill with its beak alone. It discovers that poking a stick into the anthill will cause the insects to climb out in huge numbers, providing it with an easy feast. And *then* it learns that the same trick won't work on termites, so it adjusts its behavior accordingly. Adaptation helps us apply newly learned information to adjust ourselves as conditions change.

10

Urban Wildlife

*We are kept keen on the grindstone
of pain and necessity.*

H. G. WELLS

MY FRIEND CHARLEY TOLD ME about the rising issue of urban coyotes in downtown Los Angeles.

"I was rolling the trash out to the curb," he said in his thick Louisiana accent, "and just up the street was the neighbor's cat. It looked over at me and then, within a second, a coyote came out of the alley, picked it up by the head, and took off. Now I don't care who you are, but those things have become *a problem*." The story, especially in the way he told it, with expansive gestures and a dead-eyed impression of the cat, was hilarious. I'll admit that I didn't give the pet's owner a second thought until one of my widowed congregants witnessed her beloved Havanese, a small, whitish dog, plucked from her backyard in the same way. She was devastated.

Coyotes have coexisted with us in our Orange County neighborhood for years. Never before had I heard of one entering a small, fenced-in backyard and absconding with a pet. But it was spring, the coyotes' pupping period, which meant a need for easy food and more of it.

In contrast to Los Angeles's haphazard and artistic flair, Orange County is notorious for its stringent building codes and zoning laws. Irvine, just up the road from our city, is factitiously said to only allow four shades of paint—all of them tan. Yet even here, in our planned communities, with our trimmed palm trees and timed sprinkler systems and expansive parking lots, wildlife finds a way to thrive. I've tallied more than sixty different species of birds making their way through just our little patch of backyard, plus rabbits, lizards, tree rats, mice, and one particularly freakish opossum. (Nature writer Lyanda Lynn Haupt calls these "the urban monster." No kidding.) No coyotes, yet.

We suburban and city dwellers, whether we live among the high rises in Manhattan or the sprawl of Los Angeles, the tropics of Miami or the heights of Denver, are still surrounded by wildlife. We may not have the big game of wider, wilder spaces, but there is plenty of life to be discovered if we know where to look. Seen and unseen, these birds and rodents, lizards and amphibians, insects and lagomorphs have learned to make a life among us. And wherever humans and wildlife interact, there will be consequences—some big, some small, some devastating.

The book of Acts can be read as one big story of adaptation. From the ascension of Jesus to Paul's preaching to the Romans, its arc centers on apostles of Jesus trying to figure out how in the world to navigate all of this newness. They believed that their sacrificial temple system had been fulfilled once and for all by Christ—but what was left for them in its wake? What would worship look like without all their prescribed feasts and festivals? Would it be wiser to welcome Gentiles or to keep to the ancient purity laws? How and when should they meet together in light of the burgeoning reality that Christ had died, risen, and would one day return?

They began by sharing their belongings, eating communal meals, and gathering together to sing and pray. They sought to follow the same Jesus who had risen into heaven before their eyes, leaving them no real instruction manual on what would come next. He simply told them not to leave Jerusalem, and then left them with a cryptic promise: *You will receive power when the Holy Spirit comes on you.*

How do you go back into the city to walk the same streets and sit together for a meal after you've watched your Lord and master not only rise from the dead (!) but then *ascend into heaven*? You've seen signs and miracles, but at least a little bit of you must wonder if you dreamed up the whole thing. The dead don't just *rise*. The risen don't just *ascend* up into the sky like they're riding some sort of updraft. Everything is different now. You're far from home. The religious systems that gave structure to your life since childhood are seemingly no longer in play, even as most of the Jewish world continues on exactly as it always has.

There were ten days between Jesus' departure and Pentecost. Ten long, bewildering days. The disciples replaced Judas, rounding out their number at an even twelve once again. They continued staying together in Jerusalem, as Jesus had instructed, poised for whatever was next.

And then they waited.

Adaptation does not always happen in the blink of an eye. More often it's a process. It takes time to sort through the questions and effects of change. We often need to weigh which ways we need to adapt (or not) against how those adaptations (or lack thereof) will affect us—and others.

Here's one small example: The first church I pastored was located in a small town in a very blue-collar part of the country. This culture was comfortable and familiar—I grew up in a similar place. I knew that the people valued honesty and simplicity, being "down to earth" was a high compliment while being seen to "put on airs" was its opposite. From my first days as their pastor, I chose to preach in the same simple black dress and low heels each and every week, with my only adornment a stole in the liturgical color of the season. This decision was one small way of removing distractions of class or fashion between the congregation and me. In a place where most people wore jeans to church, I was set apart as clergy, but not fancy or snobbish.

Years later, when I interviewed at my current church in Orange County, I immediately sensed that my beloved black dress and low heels would have to go. In a more appearance-oriented culture, wearing the same thing every Sunday would itself become a distraction. I traded in my black dress for a rotation of blouses paired with pencil skirts and slim pants, blazers, and cardigans. In California, I could preach in jeans, but they'd need to be stylish.

Marriage is another exercise in adaptation as we learn that the way our family of origin managed everything from dinner to laundry to holidays was completely different in our spouse's. Daryl learned to love my traditional "sunshine salad" every Christmas—orange Jello with pineapple and shredded carrots (don't make fun of it or I won't let you have any), while he taught me that authentic Mexican food goes beyond ground beef stuffed into yellow, shelf-stable taco shells from Old El Paso. We melded together his California culture with my Wisconsin German one, creating new ways of being that were unique to our own little family.

These are small examples, but all levels of change require us to adapt. The bigger the change, the bigger the adaptation. When the Palisades and Eaton fires ripped through Los Angeles, those left sifting through the ashes had to decide how they would acclimate: Would they build again? Or would they sell the land that had once held their homes and memories and move somewhere new?

"I'm too old to rebuild," one elderly woman told me, while another, younger one shared that she was already planning the fireplace she'd put into her new home. Every change is unique, and rarely is there a one-size-fits-all adaptation. We parse and pray, we watch and wait, we live and learn.

In addition, adaptation is never a one-time process. When changes come our way, we adapt and then we adapt and then we adapt again. Some of us are more adept at it than others. My kids gently rib me whenever I bring up something they loved as preschoolers as if they were still enamored with it, but adapting to the pace at which children change is tough. I can still see each of them tasting their first food, toddling around the living room, being positively over-the-moon delighted by an ice cream cone at the beach. Today our oldest son wears the same size shoes I do and will soon grow beyond those. There are days that none of the kids even *want* the ice cream cone, preferring instead a burrito or a prebiotic soda. (They're California kids, what can I say?)

When did this happen? I wonder as I watch them, their limbs stretching out, their faces losing the last vestiges of round babyhood. *When did they grow up?* I point out a sherbet-colored sunset out the car window and am met not with the happy burbles of a child equally delighted by the miracle of a uniquely painted sky but with a collective eye roll instead.

"Cool, Mom," one says. "Can I pick a song on your phone?"

I remind myself that God never changes—the same yesterday and today and forever—but also that we must. God remains constant because God is over all and through all and in all. God is everywhere, throughout time, beyond our comprehension. God holds the picture of my children as toddlers but also sees them clearly as what they are right now and what they will one day be. When I am dead and gone, God will still be steadfastly beside each one of them.

We adapt. God remains.

There is perhaps no better example of adaptation than urban birds. Yet how often we overlook our citified avian friends! It's so tempting to put the word "just" in front of their names. It's *just* a blackbird. *Just* a crow. *Just* a starling or a grackle or a gull. No matter that this gull has flown hundreds—or even *thousands*—of miles over the ocean in order to arrive at this particular shore begging for my particular french fries. It can be harder to see the magic in the birds that line our cityscapes and industrial piers, leaving piles of droppings and filling the air with their squawks. Few birders are flocking to downtown Baltimore or Los Angeles or Miami to catch a glimpse of a feral pigeon. Yet, birds that make their homes far from the woodlands and wetlands are a brilliant picture of adaptation. In a world bent upon progress, building and bulldozing, planning and developing, concrete and steel, these birds have found a way to prosper in environments that weren't originally designed for them at all.

One of my favorite stories of this radical adaptation are birds that build their dwellings out of anti-bird spikes. You've probably seen these types of avian-deterrents before—strips of sharp plastic or metal skewers attached to buildings where birds have become a nuisance. In 2021, a Dutch biologist named Auke-Florian Hiemstra was called in to investigate a very unorthodox nest atop a hospital building in Antwerp, Belgium. It turns out that a Eurasian Magpie pair had used anti-bird spikes to construct a nest, raising their tender babies within the very materials meant to keep birds from landing at all.

"They're outsmarting us," Hiemstra said. "I think it's just a brilliant comeback."

Why do some species flourish in concrete jungles while others scramble to adapt? Temperament is one factor. Shyer animals require more wilderness space and plant cover. You won't see a lynx walking through downtown Manhattan, though you will see plenty of fat, brown rats. A Virginia Rail would die of a heart attack in Times Square while a Laughing Gull would just . . . laugh. The pluckier, bolder, and more flexible a species is to begin with, the more likely it is to do well when given a new environment.

What the urban population of humans will tolerate is still another component to the success of wildlife in urban and suburban spaces. While no one loves ground squirrels stealing their lunch in Central Park, if a black bear were to wander into the theater district, someone would do something about it—and fast. To move black bears that have wandered into city spaces, most often the DNR will set a large barrel trap to contain the animal without harming it. They bait these with donuts, because if the bear needs to be moved back to the forest, at least it gets to go with frosting on its snout.

One August day years back, Daryl and the kids and I were in central California on vacation, up in Mammoth. A unique mixture of town and forest, lake and mountain, Mammoth's city limits feel fairly suburban, but you still have to empty all the food out of your car so that bears won't open it like a tin can. It's wild up there in the Sierras with its jagged granite peaks and lodgepole pines, its Red-tailed Hawks and Stellar's Jays. The air feels thin and alive; there's a tang to it that you only smell out west.

We hiked the trail around Convict Lake, a deep, spring-fed lake surrounded by towering granite mountains. It's six or seven miles outside of town, but still crowded on this August day with parking lots filled to bursting. People fished from the shore, boaters and swimmers filled the water, and a chain of horseback riders meandered high atop the lake's northern edge. The whole scene looked like a postcard for Northern California vacations.

Felicity received a Polaroid Instamatic camera that Christmas and was toting it around, adding photographer to the lengthy list of things she wanted to be when she grew up.

"Most of the jobs don't take the whole day," she told me. "So I can definitely be a doctor, a singer, a dancer, a gymnastics person, an artist, Elsa, and a photographer." At one dollar a picture, we doled out her film surreptitiously, one roll every few days. After a dip in the lake, the kids paused by the parking lot to dry off and change out of their swimsuits when we heard a loud rustle from the bushes just a few yards away.

A female mule deer, part of Mammoth's Round Valley Herd, burst from the scrub and took off down the trail to the north. The kids froze, goggle-eyed. Felicity gripped her camera with both hands but didn't move it up to her eye. None of them had ever been this close to big game in the wild before. The deer, frenzied, returned down the path and sped past us, heading south now. Its rush was close enough that I could see Felicity's blonde hair lift and settle. Then the deer spotted people on the trail ahead and spun around once more, stopping face-to-face with all of us. I realized then that we were blocking the trail down to the lake. We stood squarely between this big, panting animal and her route to safety.

"Do . . . deer . . . hurt . . . people?" Lincoln whispered.

"Just stay still," I said, calmly, knowing that yes, those hooves are sharp and mule deer, for all their spindly appearance, are much stronger and more solid than they look. There were only two exits the deer hadn't tried: straight toward us or up the stairs directly behind her to the east. Could deer even climb stairs? I didn't know for certain.

She locked eyes with us, her large ears tuned, her skin twitching. She hesitated. It was a pause of three seconds and a thousand years. The kids were statues. Daryl and I held our breath. Then the doe spun a hundred and eighty degrees and bolted up the stairs and away.

"Watch for deer," I said, and the kids laughed nervously.

"I should have taken a picture!" Felicity lamented.

The mixing of people and wildlife in places like Mammoth can offer breathtaking encounters or deadly ones. Lured into complacency by our house cat existence, we easily forget that wild animals are just that—wild. Many have adapted incredibly well to living in our midst. But the closer we come to them, the closer they will be to us. Animals deserve space and respect, both for our safety and for their own.

My only season of true city-life, not just suburbia or city-adjacent, but living in the real, gritty heart of a city was during graduate school. For one academic year I resided in a drafty apartment atop the Blarney Stone pub in Chicago's Wrigleyville, sharing space with two other recent grads. I took the "L" train to my classes on the city's north side, worked afternoons at a test prep center a few blocks from my apartment, and quickly learned the importance of things like locking doors and keeping my wits about me. The iPod my parents gifted me for graduation was lifted out of my backpack on month one. By month four the city was covered in a blizzard so thick that public transit ground to a halt, and my roommates and I were forced to make dinner with whatever we could scrounge from the liquor store across the street: pretzels, limes, chips, Sprite. Then that spring the White Sox won the World Series and South Side fans spent the hours between 11 p.m. and 4 a.m. driving circles around Wrigleyville—Cubs territory—honking and screaming.

"I don't think I'm a city girl," I told my then-boyfriend Daryl, a man born and raised in Los Angeles.

"No kidding," he said.

Like the animals, we, too, may have landscapes where we feel more or less at ease. We can adapt to many different places, of course—humans have been to the moon, the poles, and the bottom of the sea—but it's common to have a favorite spot or two that feels like *ours*. While I watched my roommates feel energized by the hustle of the city, I felt constantly off balance, overwhelmed by the pace and the noise and the crowds. I thrive in quieter, more solitary spaces. The first time my Chicago-born grandfather breathed the piney air of northern Wisconsin, he knew he was home. Sometimes change uproots us in order to bring us somewhere new that feels even more familiar than the place we left behind. Georgia O'Keefe came alive in the wilds of New Mexico after leaving the Midwest. We may realize we'd been adapting to something that didn't feel quite right for our entire lives until we finally find our true place of being.

Of course, this side of the eschaton, no place will be a seamless fit. We are all constantly adapting to our homes and neighborhoods, our communities and climates. Some places will feel almost perfect for us, others nowhere near, but within each we will discover particular longings. Something that is not *quite* right, that makes every place we live or visit feel slightly less than seamless. These are good and healthy aches. They point us to Jesus and our desire for the holy city with a tree in its center and a river running through, urban and rural, both together, where we will feel truly and finally and fully at home. Where nature, too, will be at peace.

Until then, we adapt and help one another to adapt, making a home in a world that is not our own but is nonetheless beautiful and wondrous and good.

11

Climate

The world as we have created it is a process of our thinking.
It cannot be changed without changing our thinking.

ALBERT EINSTEIN

NATURE IS BRILLIANTLY ADAPTABLE. If autumn signals a colder winter, ermine and rabbits and squirrels will grow thicker coats of fur. Tear down a bird's nest and it will build another. Moles, once decidedly forest-dwelling, have learned to thrive in suburbia where verdant lawns hide succulent earthworms, termites, and grubs. We've all seen a dandelion sprouting through a crack in the sidewalk. Against all odds, creation finds a way to carry on.

But everyone has their breaking point.

There are so many ways our robust but delicate ecosystems are being pushed to the brink because of the pain of climate change. Storms have become more frequent and severe, temperatures break records over and over again, frosts come later—or not at all. To say that this is not our fault is to miss the point entirely. Ninety-seven percent of actively publishing climate scientists agree that humans are causing climate change. It's near-impossible to find consensus that strong anywhere, but here we are. This is the bed we've made.

Contrary to popular belief, a changing climate doesn't just mean *warming*. Many weather patterns are becoming stronger and more unpredictable, including cold snaps, deep freezes, and phenomena so unusual that we have needed to invent new descriptions like "bomb cyclones," "superstorms," and "Arctic blasts."

Creation is resilient, but it is also finely calibrated. While a child with a high fever may be quite ill, one with a *very* high fever can end up brain damaged—or worse. One degree of warming or one fewer rainstorm or one more deep freeze per season may sound small, but in reality, each change taxes our planet. Eventually the camel's back is broken with just a single final straw.

It raises the question: What are we to do when facing change that is beyond our control?

Often our agency amidst changes of all sorts is far less than we would prefer. The job we've given our best efforts to suddenly informs us that we've been made redundant. Our spouse tells us that the marriage is over. A natural disaster rips through, leaving us suddenly, unexpectedly homeless. Where is God when our world careens into chaos? When all that we thought was stable and secure is shaken, rocked, and broken? We may echo the cry of the psalmist:

Why, Lord, do you stand far off?
Why do you hide yourself in times of trouble?

Nowhere may this feel more pressing than when we look closely at the state of our warming planet. What, Lord, are we to do now?

A few years ago, I attended a lecture at Calvin University's Festival of Faith and Writing by the writer and professor Marilyn McEntyre. It was titled "Writing Through a Fog of Fear."

"Be a gentle alarmist," she advised the gathered writers in the room. There are things faith and foresight tell us are too important to stop pointing toward. The scientists among us are responsible to prophetically witness to what they see coming so that the rest of us may listen to and heed their research and their warnings. We are all tasked with working for the common good for today and tomorrow and all that lies beyond. It is not too late until the apocalypse truly arrives. I appreciated

McIntyre's emphasis on doing this hard, good work of raising the alarm with tenderness. Berating, scapegoating, or shaming will rarely win us an audience, but if we tread kindly, we may yet bend the ears of the uninterested, the unbelieving, or the apathetic. Even the decided non-virtue of self-interest can potentially wake people enough to *care.*

When I was in eighth grade, my parents tried to take my sisters and me on a hike in Banff. Our packs were filled with snacks, water bottles topped off, sunscreen applied. As we stood at the trailhead adjusting our sun hats, a cheerful forest ranger came crunching down the trail.

"You may want to reconsider the hike today," he said, pointing back the way he'd come. The way we were headed. "There are grizzlies just up there. A mama with cubs." We remained frozen, slowly digesting his words. The campground we were staying at required the viewing of a fifteen-minute safety video that should have been titled, "WHEN BEARS ATTACK." My youngest sister hadn't slept for days.

"Yep, big ol' mama," the ranger concluded, tipping his hat toward us. "Well, enjoy your day!" As he disappeared around the other side of a park service truck, my sisters and I scrambled over one another to be the first back into the family van. Self-interest can be a powerful motivator.

Gentle alarmists don't despair, but neither do they let off the gas. The work is too essential. The coming pain too real. We are to steward our planet well not simply because we love God's natural world— which alone should be more than enough reason—but because creation care is one more way of spreading the good news. As Kyle Meyaard-Schaap notes in *Following Jesus in a Warming World,* "In a world racked by the devastation of rising seas, more extreme weather, and a more unpredictable and dangerous future, this means that practical steps to address the climate crisis are, in fact, acts of evangelism." Creation care is *people* care, too, another long-term strategy in following the Lord's imperative: *Learn to do right; seek justice. Defend the oppressed. Take up the cause of the Fatherless; plead the cause of the widow.* It is the poor who often feel the greatest effects of the climate crisis. Advocating for creation however we can—and living out this care in our own lives—is one more way of following Jesus whole-heartedly. One more way of slowing down our march toward this painful, global change.

The unholy split we often see between faith and science is not of God. We are beautifully entwined with the earth, ourselves just one part of God's good creation, and we ignore that symbiosis at our own peril. In her book *Braiding Sweetgrass,* Robin Wall Kimmerer quotes environmental activist Joanne Macy: "Action on behalf of life transforms. Because the relationship between self and the world is reciprocal, it is not a question of first getting enlightened or saved and then acting. As we work to heal the earth, the earth heals us." Sadly, the inverse is also true: the more we ravage the earth, the more destitute we will become.

Despair can beckon when we really learn what we've done—and continue to do—to our fragile ecosystems. Between fires on the west and east coasts (not to mention in Canada, Europe, Australia, and Mexico), hurricanes along the Eastern Seaboard, floods in the Midwest and the South, heat domes in the Pacific Northwest, worldwide droughts, and tornadoes from Oklahoma to West Virgina, there are no real climate havens remaining. The crisis knocks at each of our doors. Sooner or later, it will touch us all.

My friend Hannah sent me a video message just days after Hurricane Helene ripped through Western North Carolina—nowhere near the beach—surprising meteorologists and residents alike.

"Here's our house," she said, turning the camera to show her home on a hill. "All good here," she continued, panning across her yard. "But then we get to the other side, and, well, you can see our grocery store." It was flooded up to the roofline.

"Mommy, where are we going to buy food?" The voice of her young son came from out of frame, sounding more curious than afraid.

"Well, buddy," she said, "we are going to figure that out."

Though things may indeed look bleak at times, we are nevertheless called to work for positive change—not just for the earth but for *ourselves* who depend upon it—until there is no more opportunity remaining.

As long as it is day, we must do the works of him who sent me, Jesus reminds us. *Night is coming when no one can work.*

Some of the despair we may feel around the climate crisis can stem from the helplessness we feel around it. So much of the problem is massive and global, on a scale far out of our control. The state of our climate is largely shaped by the decisions of governments and the short-term, profit-driven choices of massive corporations. We may do what we can, recycle and grow native plants, compost and keep our the air conditioning use down, advocate for better policies for the earth and vote our consciences, but our participation is still only a small drop in a very, very big ocean. Watching national and even global choices made that will affect our air, water, plants, and animals negatively can be excruciating. And when we know it *didn't have to be this way* it can be much harder to acquiesce to difficult change.

But while the climate crisis may be relatively recent, when viewed in light of the epochs of human existence, the brutality of change outside of our control is as old as humanity itself. We need only look to Scripture, the church mothers and fathers, or the canon of literature to see that this is true. James Baldwin put it this way:

> You think your pain and your heartbreak are unprecedented in the history of the world, but then you read. It was Dostoyevsky and Dickens who taught me that the things that tormented me most were the very things that connected me with all the people who were alive, or who had ever been alive.

Artist Makoto Fujimura calls this the "common curse" a cousin to our more well-known common grace. We are united in our helplessness. United in the rawness of our need.

There is a weird sort of hope to be found in knowing that we have always existed on the razor's edge; that humanity has constantly been close to dooming itself through plague or famine, nuclear winter or global meltdown. Together we must resist the temptation to retreat into apathy or despair, and instead do all we can when we can to address the crisis—and then, somehow, courageously go on living our normal lives. This may sound strange, and yet it is ultimately the ordinary stuff of life that helps tether us to what is true and right and good.

In his 1948 essay, "On Living in an Atomic Age," C. S. Lewis writes that the first action we must take in the face of potential catastrophe is to "pull ourselves together." He continues:

> If we are all going to be destroyed by an atomic bomb, let that bomb when it comes find us doing sensible and human things— praying, working, teaching, reading, listening to music, bathing the children, playing tennis, chatting to our friends over a pint and a game of darts—not huddled together like frightened sheep and thinking about bombs. They may break our bodies (a microbe can do that) but they need not dominate our minds.

To exist in a time of climate crisis is to follow Wendell Berry's prescription to be joyful, though we've considered all the facts. This is far easier said than done. To rejoice in the face of real tragedy is possible, of course, but we are not called to fake happiness. Often the path to delight and contentment despite pain runs right through a biblical paradigm that we don't talk about as often as we should.

The road to embracing joy leads first through lament.

Before I went into the pastorate, I trained as a chaplain. At my first placement I served an Intensive Care Unit where I witnessed many, many people die. At the ripe old age of twenty-six, I was ill-equipped to handle so much suffering. I'd often end up in my supervisor's office clutching a soggy Kleenex and railing against God.

"What are the tears telling you?" Eileen used to ask me. "What are they saying?" It is in lament—the practice of crying out to God with our pain or fear or rage or sadness against the moral injury that things *are not as they should be*—that we can begin to accept the pain of unchosen, dangerous, or unstoppable change.

Scripture is filled with examples of lament, from an entire book devoted to it—Lamentations—to the psalms to the frustrated prayers from many of the leaders of our faith. Hagar laments, as does Moses, Elijah, Hannah, Paul, and so many others. We are invited to bring our deepest feelings of betrayal over the failings of our leaders, anger about our planet's current plight, sadness about what could have been, and more to the feet of Jesus.

Help, Lord, begins Psalm 12, *for no one is faithful anymore*. We can hear this cry from the ecologist weeping over a decimated forest or the college student suffering from church hurt or a meteorologist watching temperatures tick up and up and up or an epidemiologist shouting into the wind about public health. In lament, we discover that God is not afraid or unaware of our pain. That the Spirit listens and groans with us as we pour out our worries and fears. That our tears are seen, welcomed, and held.

When Daryl and I get into arguments we can't seem to easily untangle, we go back to a practice our premarital counselors taught us nearly two decades ago. It's called "Speaker-Listener." One person holds an object—usually a book because we always have one of those within arm's reach—and only that person is allowed to speak.

Say Daryl goes first. He'd state his part of the argument in a few sentences and my job would be to listen carefully. When he finishes, I will then paraphrase back to him what he said to me. Not only does this show him that I've been listening, but it allows him to hear the echo and make any adjustments he needs. When we're heated or sad, often our words come out more jumbled than we realize. Then, when he's satisfied that I've truly heard him, it is my turn to speak and he will pass the book to me. We often need to repeat the cycle four or five times in a single argument before we begin to find our way through. The whole thing is as dorky as you can imagine, but do you know what? It *works.*

Here's the interesting part though: Often it is just in being *heard* that we begin to relax. That the temperature begins to cool. We have said the words we needed to say, and another has witnessed and repeated them to us. This is part of the relief of lament. When we pray what has been weighing us down, driving us to madness, dragging us toward despair, God *listens.* And there is profound healing in the act of being heard. It doesn't usually solve everything, but it is a solid start.

We all have much to lament when it comes to the climate crisis, but other, less global changes may drive us to lament as well. God does not bar us from bringing requests about anything, big or small. It's a minor tragedy when we decide not to open our hearts in lament because we've decided we *shouldn't* feel a certain way about something, or that it's too inconsequential to bother the Almighty with. God is eager to hear our cries, whatever their size. Ready, always, to receive our prayer.

Nearly every change will bring grief along with it, good change as well as bad. We may rejoice at our wedding but lament the loss of the single life we enjoyed or former roommates we loved. We can delight in the birth of a child but mourn our lost nights of sleep. We might feel thrilled to retire, but then miss the camaraderie of the office break room. God instructs us to rejoice, but not as a replacement for the vital practice of lament.

Both are part of weathering change.

"2012 has not been good to us," a beloved congregant once told me as I sat in her kitchen. Her son had just been diagnosed with an aggressive cancer, and I'd come to offer prayer. Two weeks earlier, I'd stood in the same room as we watched the coroner wheel her husband out on a gurney to the waiting hearse. A week after that I'd officiated his funeral.

There is nothing to say in these moments, nothing that will lift the pain or fix the unfixable problem, but I was there to listen and to witness her lament. Together we looked out the picture window at a giant maple tree, its branches bare against the iron gray of a winter sky.

"I don't know what to do next," she said after a lengthy period of silence. "But I guess my son being sick will keep me busy."

At the church I currently serve in California, we celebrate a service of memories every November, a time for those who are mourning the loss of loved ones to sing hymns and hear a short message about weathering grief during the holidays. The high point of the service is when each participant is invited to come forward, light a candle, and speak the name of their loved one into a microphone for everyone to hear. Some have lost a spouse or a parent or a child that very year; others come to remember someone who died a long, long time ago.

At the reception afterward, sweets and coffee and tears flow.

"I miss him too," I'll tell widows, laying a gentle hand on their shoulders. "I miss her too," I'll say to the widowers. In those moments, acknowledging a loss, the incredible effort it takes to adapt to a new hole in the heart, a new silence in the home, is one small way to honor the dignity of us all. We have not forgotten. God will not forget.

Sometimes we adapt only because we have to. There is no choice set before us. We all face changes we did not choose; disasters we did not welcome. We will watch as our planet heats and spins, approaching a tipping point that may send us toward our earthly doom. The grief can be crushing. Yet here, too, we will find the Lord. Scripture describes Jesus as *a man of sorrows, and acquainted with grief.*

We are not alone in the pain of change. The knowledge of this closeness will not solve our suffering, but it can make it less lonely, less isolating. James Baldwin continued his reflection on the universality of suffering by acknowledging the way our pain can connect us to one another: "Only if we face these open wounds in ourselves can we understand them in other people," he wrote. There is grace in the ache, not only for us but for those our lives will touch.

We cannot look away. But we must also keep looking up.

12

Winter

Maybe the hardest notion to accept
about winter is that it is so alive.

PETER J. MARCHAND

LATE ONE DECEMBER, Daryl and the kids and I made the long trek east and north to Wisconsin to visit my family for the New Year's holiday. It would be a whole family reunion as my sisters and their families drove over to join us from their places in Minnesota. Our kids were practically levitating with excitement because Aunt Caitlyn had promised to bring *hockey skates.*

After opening the last remaining presents of Christmas, my brother-in-law trekked down to the lake to check the ice and found it thick enough to bear weight. The winter had been cold, unseasonably cold, but largely snowless. The lake was perfect. Our kids poured out of the house and ran down through the yard with the anticipation of trying something they never had before. Together we laced up on the dock next to their cousins and stepped out onto frozen waters smooth as glass. My parents live on the largest chain of inland lakes anywhere in the world. We could skate for miles. We could skate forever.

When the wind kicked up, tiny dry bits of snow like fat grains of sugar would dance across the surface, leaving wisps and ghost trails. The kids fell and stood back up and pushed plastic lawn chairs around and fell again and stood back up again and burst into squeals of joy.

I spent the first eighteen years of my life in Wisconsin, and another five pastoring there, but I'd never seen this combination of elements. The lake was frozen so hard, so snowless, so smooth. Before we had kids, we'd shovel off a small rink some years, the heavy, wet snow shrinking our planned efforts from Olympic-sized to living room–sized. We'd bring out hockey sticks and elbow each other into the snow drifts. Many years it was too wet or too warm or even too bitterly cold to skate at all. But on this particular year, we could sail around the treelined bends, across from one neighbor's pier to the one beyond and the one beyond that, all the way from one lake to the next.

Every winter is different. Some, like that one, are magic. Others are ethereal in their beauty or so mundane that the days seem utterly indistinguishable from one another, blending into a giant gray nothingness. Occasionally, a winter is so brutal that by its end you half-believe that hell itself must be cold. But like the mythical snowflakes, every one unique, the winter season enters and stays and retreats differently year upon year, each a particular blessing and grace and trial.

Some change will smack us in the face, like the snap of cold. Our life was on a path, a trajectory. All was summer, abundance. But then, suddenly, everything is different. Winter has come.

Back in 2006, Daryl and I were newlyweds, living in a Chicago apartment so tiny we could vacuum the entire thing without ever once unplugging the appliance. One snowy day, we sat by the window and watched the mailbox on the street two floors below. We'd heard from a friend that very morning who had just received an acceptance to the PhD program at Princeton Theological Seminary. Daryl's graduate school professors assured him that he was a shoo-in. We were certain his acceptance was on its way at any moment.

We had staked our entire future on this program. I would study for my MDiv while he earned his dream PhD. After graduation, I would go into service to the church and he would enter the academy as a professor. We would be serving God in our own unique ways together, learning our craft in the same hallowed halls and with the same cadre of professors. We could even take a few overlapping classes, if we wanted. Three years hence, I'd be ready to take a pastoral call. A few beyond that, and he'd be ready to don the title of doctor and begin teaching. It was all so perfect.

Plus, we knew that God would be on our side. We wanted to give our lives to the church and the theological academy, seeking to love God with our minds and trusting Jesus with our financial future. Why *wouldn't* the Lord bless our desire to serve in this way? More than one well-meaning family member pointed out all the more lucrative options before us—business or law school, entering the working world to climb its ladders—but we were steadfast in our decision. Besides, I was no stranger to working odd jobs to make ends meet. I'd served as a bar pianist in high school, cleaned the student center's climbing wall in college, and paid rent during my master's degree by working as an adjunct instructor at a university. One summer, I got hired as Grocery Store Demo Girl, a boon when I got to take home leftover waffles but an exercise in public humiliation when I had to spend eight straight hours, minus one half-hour lunch break, demonstrating the Clorox Bath Wand™.

Daryl and I set our faces to the future and waited eagerly for news of his acceptance. With that in hand, our vocational journey could begin.

The mail carrier came at last, and Daryl ran down in his jeans and T-shirt, too excited to even throw on a coat. He pounded up the stairs with the envelope so we could open it together.

"It's thin," he said, a flicker of doubt in his eyes.

"I'm sure they'll send more materials later," I said. "This will just be the welcome." We crouched together on our living room sofa, my arm slung over his shoulders. "Open it!" I said.

He slowly slit open the envelope and lifted out a letter.

"Dear Daryl," he began, reading it aloud. "Thank you for your application. After careful consideration, we are declining to make you an offer of acceptance this year." We both froze. All the oxygen had been sucked from the room, a howling vortex vacuuming up our entire futures. I choked out a little gasp. Daryl quickly set down the letter, ran to the bathroom, and threw up.

Animals feature brilliant adaptations to winter's hardships. Grouse burrow down into the snow where temperatures are slightly warmer and they will receive protection from the wind. White-tailed deer develop thick coats and store a large percentage of body fat as insulation. Wood frogs make their winter home under thin leaf litter, a scant protection from the cold. Yet their bodies are capable of cooling to very low temperatures, a form of terrestrial hibernation that withstands total freezing. Their metabolism slows to a crawl; their hearts even stop beating! In spring, they thaw, reanimating, frog-shaped ice cubes. Each living creature adapts to winter's threat in its own way.

In her book *Wintering*, Katherine May describes how flora and fauna respond to the challenges of the coldest season:

> Plants and animals don't fight the winter; they don't pretend it's not happening and attempt to carry on living the same lives that they lived in the summer. They prepare. They adapt. They perform extraordinary acts of metamorphosis to get them through. Winter is a time of withdrawing from the world, maximizing scant resources, carrying out acts of brutal efficiency and vanishing from sight; but that's where the transformation occurs. Winter is not the death of the life cycle, but its crucible.

It is in winter that nature's many creatures and plants survive or perish. For many, it is their greatest test.

As difficult as winter is, there is no one right way to weather the changes it brings. Peter J. Marchand notes in *Life in the Cold*, "The forces shaping life in snow country often evoke different strategies, none of which solve all problems, but each of which serves a particular organism in terms of its own role in the scheme of things." As nature has evolved to tackle winter, each plant and animal has learned to approach it differently, uniquely solving some of winter's problems but also leaving them open to others.

Migratory birds escape winter's worst temperatures, but migration is a taxing and dangerous enterprise in and of itself. Hibernating creatures are unaware of the darkest months of winter, but hibernation isn't simply sleeping away the time. In fact, most warm-blooded animals have to rise out of their taxing hibernation state multiple times each month, in part so that they can warm up their bodies enough to get some restful sleep. And animals that neither hibernate nor migrate are faced with only one remaining option: resist.

When we draw parallels between the wintering of animals and plants and our own lives, we do not speak only of seasons. For us, metaphorical winter may be any time of brutal, difficult change. A death in the family brings winter. A health crisis. The loss of a friendship or a job. Family estrangement. Leaving a church or moving away from a beloved home. We will all face personal winters.

Then there are the winters of our communities, brutal times of scarcity and want, of great uncertainty, of violence and darkness that extend to whole cities or nations or even continents. Some of these chilling seasons are ongoing today. Others we read of in the pages of our Scriptures. The liturgical passage that follows the joy of Christ's birth is Herod's murder of the innocents. The early church was founded amidst martyrdom and bloody persecution. Closer to home and more recently, great swaths of American Indian tribes were forcibly removed from their land in order to make room for white settlers. The great evil of slavery stained our country in ways we must still reckon with. Today's politicians spread misinformation and disinformation like confetti, leaving the rest of us hunting for truth in a disorienting storm of colorful lies. There have been many winters in this world. There will be more winters still to come.

In Germany in the late 1920s, a great chill descended. With the Nazi party's rise to power, horrific persecution against the Jewish people ramped up immediately, as did crackdowns on dissidents, deviants, and those who did not toe the line of the corrupt state faith. Pastors and churches who regurgitated the party line were largely left alone, but those who spoke up about the truth that nationalism and discipleship were not proper bedfellows and that their primary allegiance was to Christ were punished, and often severely.

As this persecution rose, a twenty-five-year-old Lutheran pastor named Dietrich Bonhoeffer retreated from Germany to serve a German-speaking church in London. While it was becoming clear that nowhere on the European continent was completely insulated from the Nazi Party's violence and Hitler's power grabs, London was safer than Germany itself.

When Bonhoeffer's friend and mentor, the prolific Swiss theologian Karl Barth, heard of Bonhoeffer's new position, he wrote him a scathing letter: "You must . . . think of only one thing, that you are a German, that the house of your church is on fire, that you know enough to be able to help and that you must return." Barth instructed Bonhoeffer to return by the very next ship, and Bonhoeffer, chastened by the elder theologian's words, did come back—though not for sixteen more months.

By 1935, Barth had been exiled for refusing to sign the Oath of Loyalty to Hitler. Noted Barth, "Granted, I did not refuse to give the official oath, but I stipulated that I could be loyal to the Führer only within my responsibilities as an Evangelical Christian." Unsurprisingly, this response did not fly with the German Chancellor, and Barth was forced to flee the country.

Barth and Bonhoeffer adapted differently to the challenges of serving the European church in these dark hours. Barth was older and more established, a bookish and bombastic scholar. Bonhoeffer was younger and more untested, still growing into his gravitas as a theologian, but also more of a calculated risk taker. I see echoes of Paul and Peter in the two of them.

Bonhoeffer's writings have been standard fare for seminary students for three quarters of a century, and rightly so. A pastor's pastor, Bonhoeffer's works are a masterclass on following Jesus when political and social conditions begin to deteriorate. When winter comes.

United in their desire to serve the Confessing Church and keep Christ at the center, Barth and Bonhoeffer used their unique gifts and callings to stand for truth amidst a regime of propaganda, lies, and violence.

It would cost one his life.

Fourteen years after his return to Germany, Bonhoeffer was murdered in Flossenburg concentration camp for his role in Operation 7, a plan to smuggle Jews into Switzerland; helping Confessing Church pastors evade military service; the plot to kill Hitler; and being a general bee in the bonnet of the Nazi regime.

His death came two weeks before the camp was liberated by the allies on April 23, just as spring began to arrive.

Many of winter's hazards are hidden: the thin spot on the lake ice, the storm brewing in the Arctic, the acorn cache so carefully curated that is then raided by another. But we also know that winter will come. We can count on it. Its arrival may shock us, but the knowledge that we will face it should not. Seasons of difficult change are inevitable for each one of us. We just don't always know *when* they will take place.

One of my favorite characters in the Nativity story is Anna. She and Simeon tend to get short shrift after the seasonal focus on shepherds and angels and even wise men (whom scholars tend to agree didn't even arrive to meet Jesus until around *two years* after his birth!). Our parish associate, John, lamented this year that no kids ever clamor to play Anna or Simeon in Christmas pageants. In fact, I've never seen them included at all. We may pay these elders little mind, but they deserve our time. Their stories are profound.

A prophetess, we are told by the Gospel of Luke that Anna was married for seven years before her husband's death and was then a widow until the age of eighty-four. For decades, she never left the temple "but worshiped night and day, fasting and praying." I can scarcely imagine the life of this woman. In biblical times, becoming a widow often also meant becoming destitute. Women couldn't own property, so if there weren't male relatives able to step in and provide after the death of a spouse, their future prospects were bleak. Remarriage was one of their only hopes for financial provision.

Yet Anna hadn't taken this path, whether by choice or not being chosen, and instead she resides in the temple, worshiping, fasting, and praying. We may wonder if her fasting was a decision or a necessity, a result of her poverty. Yet either way, God sustained her through this long winter. Her life was not the one she had hoped for, nor the one any of us would have chosen. It had chosen her, as difficult changes so often do. Her choice came in what to do with the hand she'd been dealt.

These many years on, we meet Anna at the temple. She is still there. Still worshiping. Still praying. Her life has taken on the rhythms of the temple, adapting to the contours of its liturgical seasons. Her whole world has been subsumed by the things of God.

Anna likely knew Simeon, an older man who also frequented that holy place. Perhaps the two of them had conversations about the promise the Holy Spirit revealed to him, that Simeon trusted he would not die before he had seen the Lord's Messiah. Perhaps Anna had begun keeping an eye on Simeon, hoping that if he met this Christ, she may have a chance to encounter him too.

Then, one day, Anna overhears Simeon singing: *Sovereign Lord, as you have promised, you now dismiss your servant in peace. For my eyes have seen your salvation.* She sees him standing with a young couple, a man and a woman, holding an eight-day-old baby. They must be at the temple for his ritual circumcision. It is not unusual to see babies on their eighth day, for this is the time prescribed by Jewish law.

Anna moves to them. At age eighty-four, she has watched empires rise and fall. She has witnessed tragedy in this temple—weeping mothers and grieving fathers. She has watched poor widows put their brave, meager offerings into the coffers and the rich show off their flashy clothing. She has seen the evidence of more blood sacrifices than she can count. She has kept praying. Kept fasting. Kept worshiping.

And today she will meet the Messiah.

Anna goes to Mary and Joseph, gives thanks to God, and then speaks—as a prophet is wont to do—about what will happen next. The redemption of Jerusalem. The redemption of all of her long, painful years.

And our own.

Winter does not last forever. Eventually the thaw will come, the freeze will end, the spring will arrive, warming the earth. Daryl and I spent the rest of that devastating PhD rejection day so many years ago curled up together reading Sherlock Holmes stories. Sometimes cozy comfort literature is just the thing to help accommodate us to winter's shock.

Then, a few days later, he received an email from a kind professor. The scholar had seen his application and noted that it was very, very strong. He apologized that Princeton couldn't offer Daryl a placement that year. And then the kicker: He encouraged Daryl to transfer his application to their MDiv program instead.

"You would have an even better chance of acceptance in our PhD program after an MDiv with us," he wrote.

Daryl and I spent the next few days torn between the pain of his rejection and the glimmer of this new possibility. Daryl was heartened that this professor had noticed him, but miffed at his suggestion of an MDiv.

"That's a pastoral degree," he told me. "That's your road, not mine. I have no interest in becoming a pastor." Still, since we were going to be spending three years in New Jersey anyway while I earned my own MDiv, at least enrolling this program would keep Daryl in the academy. It could help him network with folks who might help him on his next round of applications. We decided to take the leap.

Over the next two years, Daryl finished his MDiv and then was indeed accepted to Princeton's PhD program—though he ended up choosing to study at Vanderbilt instead. Still, that day on the couch was a turning point for us both, the start of a span of years where I began to see Daryl's pastoral gifting and he began to experience an unexpected tug into formal ecclesial life. Even after finishing his PhD, he never went into the academy. Instead, he recently celebrated his first full decade of ordained ministry, pastoring alongside me at our church here in California.

Winter can turn everything we knew upside down. The bubbling brook freezes solid. The trees lose their leaves. The birds fly south or hunker down. All is hushed and still. The world looks dead and buried.

But winter can also be the gateway to a surprising spring.

13

Molting

We are not exempt from the desert wanderings—
but how else would we be transformed?

DEBBIE BLUE

MOLTING IS NOT a dignified process. Feathers fall out in singles or clumps at dedicated times once or twice or three times per year, leaving birds disheveled. Delicate hummingbirds appear as though they've been in a blender; gallant owls look like they've had one too many pints at the pub. And as birds lose the feathers on their heads, they begin to look positively reptilian, like their dinosaur ancestors of old. Molting birds are odd, messy, and bedraggled. Yet despite its indignities, molting is an essential transformation for any healthy bird.

Ornithologists have a phrase for why birds need to molt: *feather wear*. Feathers aren't alive, of course, they're made of beta-keratin and of similar structure to our own hair or fingernails. But with all the activity involved in just being a bird—flight and feeding, breeding and nesting, escape from predators and sheltering from bad weather—their feathers get pretty beat up. While flight feathers are big, strong, and obviously important, even the smallest of feathers help with insulation and temperature regulation. They all need replacing every so often— usually between every three and twelve months. Old feathers fall out and new ones—pinfeathers—slowly push through the surface of the skin and unfurl to dry in the breezes and the sun. Molting is essential, even if it isn't beautiful. Damaged feathers must be replaced.

It takes a great deal of energy for a bird to create new feathers, expending precious calories in order to form them. But the loss of old and the creation of new must take some inner fortitude, too, because not only does it leave them less protected from temperature fluctuations and even, in some cases, briefly unable to fly—they look very silly too.

Good thing molting season is nowhere near breeding season. It would be hard for a molting male to impress the ladies.

Physical changes can be hard to weather well. After the birth of each of our three babies I felt wildly out of control for months, everything swollen and tender and leaking. I wanted to hole up until I could fit back into my regular pants and present my polished, put-together self to the world once more. Yet life will not often stand still in light of our fragilities. We must brave the high school halls despite our acne or we show up to the boardroom even with our arm in a sling. In an age of Zoom, we can still make it to the scheduled meeting with a virus in tow. (Oh joy.)

But sometimes physical changes take us down to the point where life *does* stop moving forward. There are times when we literally cannot continue as we always have. We listen to the soft animal of our body crying *uncle* and we say, "Okay. I hear you. Let's push pause." I rushed back to work six weeks after the birth of our eldest and quickly discovered that I was in no condition to be running meetings or offering pastoral care. My body was still finding its new equilibrium after the brutal changes that accompanied bringing a new life into the world. Many physical transitions require time and gentleness; they cannot be sped along. Others will force permanent change—on the other side, things will never be the same.

In Scripture, physical maladies most often show up in the text right before miraculous acts of healing. The man born blind is given sight. A dead girl is raised to life. A group of friends pick up a mat to bring their paralyzed companion to Jesus, and when the crowds won't let them through, they open up a hole in the roof and lower him down.

Jesus sees the man, praises the faith of his friends, and then commands the man to stand, pick up his mat, and walk.

Yet our injuries and ailments most often don't resolve miraculously. We still have to wear the brace, use the wheelchair, put in the hearing aids. We take the medication so that we don't have another heart attack or go into diabetic ketoacidosis or struggle to focus in class. The biblical stories of being made well—seizures stopped, sight restored, limbs straightened—can start to seem taunting, even cruel. Worse yet, other people of faith can add shame to our pain.

"We need to pray that out of you," a pastor's wife once told me when I let her know of my severe gluten intolerance. The insinuation that I hadn't already been praying—begging—God for years to take away this expensive, socially awkward, and medically frustrating ailment irked me, but so did her concept of God as cosmic vending machine. *Ask and you shall receive,* Jesus says in the Sermon on the Mount, but we will all ask for many things that we'll never receive. What gives?

Catherine of Siena was an Italian Catholic mystic in the fourteenth century who began having visions of Christ as a young girl. Burdened by physical suffering as well as her desire for more complete holiness, Catherine received a vision in which Jesus seemed to offer a balm to her in her suffering. "Very pleasing to Me, dearest daughter, is the willing desire to bear every pain and fatigue, even unto death," Jesus told her. "Therefore bear yourselves with manly courage." Catherine took his words to heart, finding a particular solace within even the ache of her frail body.

I do not know why so many of our trials and maladies do not end with miraculous healing but instead continue for years or decades or even whole lifetimes, but I suspect it has something to do with the intimacy of dependence. There is a unique closeness we might experience with Jesus when our physical limitations and bodily discomforts bring us, time and again, to our knees. The molting bird must treat itself with even more gentleness and care, adapting to a new reality of frailty and dependence—however long.

Have you ever seen a bird wearing an anklet? Look closely and sometimes—rarely, but sometimes—you'll notice a little band of metal
around a leg. Grab your binoculars, and you might see numbers
stamped on the band, too.

Microbiologist Janet Hill noticed a banded Blue Jay in her backyard
one spring day in 2016. When it returned the next year and the one
after that, she got curious and grabbed her camera. "I just sat out on
my deck, and I started taking pictures of this bird's leg and over a
period of several days—I took a *lot* of photos because every time . . .
[the band] would be rotated slightly differently. And one night, I finally got it," she told me.

Janet looked up the number and discovered that the jay had been
banded in 2014 by Stuart and Mary Houston, legendary bird-banders
that lived just a few blocks from her home. Janet named the bird Mary,
in honor of her banders. Waiting for Mary to return became a beloved
spring ritual. As of the writing of this book, the bird continues to come
back to Janet's yard. Mary is at least ten years old now, a very ripe old
age for a Blue Jay. Without the identifying band, Janet would have
struggled to track her, since birds of this species are nearly identical to
one another. The band told the story.

There are many reasons ornithologists band birds, from studying
their migratory patterns to identifying breeding habits to discerning
which individuals within a larger population remain healthy. The
methods for capturing birds differ with each species' size and temperament, but for small songbirds, scientists tend to prefer mist nets.

Mist nets are just what they sound like—large nets woven with very
fine-gauge line, virtually invisible to flying birds. Bird-banders set
them up in transitional spaces like tree lines where birds will most
often be traveling back and forth. Then they wait. When a bird flies
into the net, its wings and body become entangled, holding it there
until a person comes to gently remove, band, and study it. The birds

are weighed and measured, their bodies inspected for signs of disease. Their feathers offer clues that can help banders determine their stage of molt as well as their age. Then they are released. This is all done with the proper training and permits, mind you, so don't get any ideas about trying it on your own. (Though many universities and organizations need seasonal help and are eager to train new recruits!)

"The ethics of what you're doing is always at the forefront," ornithologist Dan Baldassarre told me. "You are literally taking a bird's life in your hands. It's a big privilege. If you're going to put the bird through that stress, it's got to be for a good reason, and you have to be doing it safely and ethically." I asked him whether there were any types of birds that struggled more than others with the banding process. He told me,

> Most birds, especially passerines—your sort of small-to-medium birds—are pretty docile when you get them in the hand. But there are exceptions. Most woodpeckers are not very happy to be held onto. You can envision [it]—their whole life history is just slamming their beaks into objects. They're happy to do that to your finger. . . . There are a couple of others that are notorious around banders. Northern Cardinals! Boy, I didn't appreciate how . . . strong their beaks were! The first couple of times I went out catching them they just destroyed my knuckles. But I don't fault them for it.

I love knowing that different birds react differently to becoming stuck in a mist net and handled by a bander. Some are patient, others impatient. Some go quietly, accepting their uncertain fate. Others try to take their pound of flesh on the way out.

Change? Cardinals do not consent.

Fighting against inevitable change will not improve our experience of it. We all remember the many horrors of puberty, don't we? Nobody escaped it unscathed. I turned immediately to tears when my mother informed me that I would bleed for five or six days every month for the next *thirty to forty years*. After drying my eyes, I decided that I simply would not acquiesce to this madness. Denial can be a wonderful comfort until you find yourself stranded in a public bathroom with no sanitary supplies.

Birds have no say in how and when they will lose their feathers, and we may learn something from their stoic acceptance of and placid adaptivity to these changes. Nonmigratory, Northern Cardinals stay put in winter, building up body fat and puffing up their feathers up for insulation against temperatures that can dive into the subzero range. They sing a dozen different songs or so, but it is their chirp call that is most well-known. It sounds metallic and cartoonish, sort of like a Star Wars blaster: *pew-pew! Pew pew pew!* Cardinals are beloved by Midwesterners who adore them for the cheery pop of color they offer during long, gray winters.

But perhaps no bird is as awkward in its molting stage as the Northern Cardinal. Naturalists and wildlife veterinarians regularly field calls by concerned citizens who have spotted these birds in the early fall, shedding their worn plumage in time to sprout newer, healthier feathers for winter. These backyard birders believe that they may have discovered a new species of bird, but one that is probably in need of immediate medical attention. It's no wonder—molting Northern Cardinals do not look much like cardinals. They barely look like songbirds at all. Definitely not healthy ones. When the red feathers of their head and crest fall out to make room for new growth, often shedding nearly all at once, cardinals look like Darth Maul after he lost to Obi-Wan. The shiny black skin of a molted cardinal's caps holds an orange beak that now looks much too big for its face. Their eyes glitter and bulge. They look like tiny red vultures. (Take a second and look up molting cardinals on the internet. I promise you won't be sorry.)

Their beauty will return, pinfeathers pushing their way through neck and cap and back. Molting is messy, yes, but as Ted Floyd notes in *How to Know the Birds*, it "is also ordered and logical and eminently sensible." In the meantime, as they wait for their feathers to come back in, the cardinals can do nothing but bide their time. Some changes cannot be rushed.

At the end of the book of Jeremiah, the Israelites have been marched into exile, carried off by the Babylonians and forced to live out their days in a strange land among unfamiliar people. The food is different, the climate unfamiliar. They miss their fields and vineyards. Worst of all, the Babylonians do not worship the God of the Israelites. Desperate to return home, the Israelites begin doing what most of us would do—preparing to get out of there.

With one foot out the door and their hearts filled with repentance, they exist within painful uncertainty, wanting to go but forced to stay. They don't want to adapt to this new, unfamiliar place. It isn't home and it never will be.

Then God speaks.

Seek the peace and prosperity of the city, God tells them through Jeremiah, their reviled prophet. *If it prospers, you too will prosper*. It's the ancient Hebraic version of our modern clichés: "Wherever you are, be all there," or "Bloom where you're planted." God asks them to unload their carts and unpack their baskets, even as they continue to hold the hope of returning to their homeland at any moment. *Patience*, God counsels. *This will take time.*

There is great biblical precedent in balancing deep yearning for something else, something better, with the hard work right in front of us. Change can be sudden, immediate, but just as often it is drawn out far longer than we'd prefer and feels more unpleasant than we would like. Though the Israelites were in exile for seventy years, God never abandoned them in the in-between. Nor will we be abandoned.

I learned recently that cardinals were named after the officers of the Catholic Church rather than the other way round, their colors inspiring the connection. In folklore, cardinals are often synonymous

with confidence, a feathered reminder to turn our attention heavenward to the one who never changes.

Molting isn't very dignified. Physical ailments, unplanned moves,
or any change we wouldn't choose for ourselves can be a steep hill to
climb. And yet when we can learn to practice patience with ourselves,
giving space for the grief of change, we can begin to find a new normal.
A new way through. Adaptation.

Feather wear comes for us all. But then, so does hope.

14

Water

The wise adapt themselves to circumstances,
as water molds itself to the pitcher.

CHINESE PROVERB

THE REALITY THAT ICE FLOATS is a game-changer. It is an incredibly rare behavior for a chemical compound. Nearly all other solids are denser than their liquid forms and, therefore, will sink to the bottom of their own liquids. Without the unique property of water's changing density, lakes would freeze from the bottom up, killing the wildlife within them. The mechanism for the density shift in water creates one of the most fascinating phenomena in winter lakes: As autumn turns colder, lakes will "turn over," a process involving "the mixing of surface and bottom waters that redistributes resources in the aquatic environment." This overturn happens when cooling water— denser than warm—reaches its maximum density at 39.2 degrees Fahrenheit. As it continues to cool, it then becomes lighter, rising back to the top where it will eventually turn to ice.

I remember watching this turnover reverse itself each spring on Yellow Birch Lake. When the surface ice had melted, my dad would grab a neighbor and together they would wade out to install our little wooden pier, its pine boards painted the color of redwood. My sisters and I would stand out on it in the days that followed, watching as the waters—nearly clear to the bottom in the earliest days of spring—turned murky with sediment when the coldest layer of water on top had warmed and the lake performed its spring turnover.

We can think of situations—in nature, but also in our own lives and communities and even our world—where such a shakeup has occurred. Suddenly up is down, left is right, and we are left unmoored and drowning, surprised to find ourselves at the bottom of a metaphorical lake. Covid-19 was one such global overturn—industry ground to a halt, schools shuttered, hospitals overwhelmed, mass illness and death all around. There have been many others. There will be more to come.

"We are becoming enemies to people who used to depend on us as friends," an acquaintance in the foreign service told me as a new administration took a sledgehammer to formerly stable diplomatic relationships. "It is very painful to watch."

Smaller, more personal turnovers can be just as devastating as global ones to the individual people that they touch. The summer after my junior year of college, I learned that my friend Sam died in a kayaking accident in the icy waters of Lake Superior. When I got the news, I gasped and then—to my horror—a laugh escaped. It was not funny, of course, it was not funny in the slightest, but it was so *absurd*. Twenty-three-year-olds who had formerly captained the basketball team, who were strong swimmers, who were not only athletic but kind too? They didn't just *drown*. I could still picture him, all 6'8" of him, dancing with his girlfriend at our high school prom. She barely grazed five feet, so she had dragged a chair to the middle of the dance floor, standing on it in her bare feet, her arms around his neck, and his around her waist.

But somehow it was true. Sam was gone. He is still gone. And in that moment, everything turned over. I learned that these things can happen to any of us. That the healthiest among us could, at any moment, vanish into the depths. I watched grief dance in the eyes of my young friends as we gathered in my childhood church in our black dresses and hand-me-down suits, the first time that most of us had been touched by the death of a healthy peer. We shared stories about

Sam, all while pondering how we might adapt to this frightening and capricious new world without him.

Life teeters on the edge of a cataract, every day bringing with it the chance that we may spill over onto the jagged rocks below. That this is the only place it can be lived.

Over 97 percent of the earth's water exists in its oceans. The remaining 3 percent is split between 2 percent found in icebergs and polar ice caps and less than 1 percent in lakes, rivers, ponds, and groundwater. The sea is a majestic and masterful thing, beautiful and wild, sometimes peaceful and other times incredibly violent. In Scripture, it is often used as a symbol of evil and chaos with its dark, unpredictable, unplumbable depths.

"Beyond there be dragons," noted one medieval map, pointing to the edge of the known sea.

The fearsomeness of the ocean can be a comfort, too, with its immensity and power helping to drown out the relentless drumbeat of our own problems. One day in April, finishing the edits on *Looking Up,* a book about birds, hope, and the death of my maternal grandfather, I received news that my paternal grandfather had died back in Michigan. I was on my way to work when the text came in and my inner autopilot kicked on. I continued the drive, unlocked my church office, set up my computer, and started to comb through my inbox. An hour later, Daryl found me at my desk, staring at a blinking cursor on a blank screen.

"You okay?" he asked. He'd been included on the text thread about my grandfather's death.

"I don't think I can be here," I told him, the reality of the loss starting to settle onto my shoulders brick by brick, pressing me down into my chair. Into the carpet. Into the earth.

"Then don't be," he said. "Go wherever you need to go." I got in the car and drove north, not sure where I was headed until I pulled up to the Bolsa Chica Reserve, a tidal estuary with whipping winds where the ocean surges inland, making islets and filling marshes. There, at the edge of the world, I received from the Lord dozens of Brown Pelicans, a Snowy Egret, a Great Blue Heron, and too many terns to count. I watched them and slowly, ever so slowly, began to find my breath again.

A giant had fallen. And here on the edge of the continent, more than two thousand miles away from where my grandmother grieved in Michigan, surrounded by the piercing calls of terns and the inexorable pull of the tide, I mourned him.

Water will seek the lowest point, following gravity's pull down everything from waterfalls to neighborhood streams to flooded basements. In Margaret Atwood's *The Penelopiad*, a retelling of *The Odyssey* from Penelope's perspective, the mother puts it this way,

> Water does not resist. Water flows. When you plunge your hand into it, all you feel is a caress. Water is not a solid wall, it will not stop you. But water always goes where it wants to go, and nothing in the end can stand against it. Water is patient. Dripping water wears away a stone. Remember that, my child. Remember you are half water. If you can't go through an obstacle, go around it. Water does.

It is this flexibility that allows water to do its work, adapting to a myriad of changing circumstances. It flows but it also evaporates, turning into vapor that can travel over mountain ridges and across deserts, moving from continent to continent. It condenses into clouds that sail the globe, bringing rain and snow, sleet and hail. When faced with blockades, water will always find a way.

It is water's persistent, gentle seeking that I want to cultivate in my own heart when it comes to change. I fluctuate from bulldozer to couch potato, knocking things down or else retreating from them, when really it is emulating the curious power of water—dripping, flowing, running, streaming, both gentle and relentless—that will help most. When obstacles arise—as they always will—I want to learn how to find my flow.

My sisters and I grew up with rigid rules around dating and courtship. We weren't allowed to go out with boys until we turned sixteen, and then only in groups. We weren't permitted to attend any school dances—even without dating—until we were sophomores in high school. I don't begrudge my parents these decisions. I can see where they were coming from—having kids is scary and watching those kids hit puberty is scarier still. (Plus, it was the '90s when the evangelical subculture's teaching on protecting the kids from The World™ by retreating from it was at its peak.)

"Don't have sex or you will get pregnant *and die,*" says the character played by Tim Meadows in the movie *Mean Girls,* and that was the basic message I received. When it comes to issues of burgeoning adolescent sexuality, many adults prefer to err on the side of terrified caution. When faced with unsettling change, it's tempting to erect rigid boundaries and set inflexible rules in excess. *Why take any chances?* we reason. *The consequences could be so severe!*

Still, this prohibition turned dating into a forbidden object, and these sorts of objects have a way of becoming even more enticing. Dating became all I could think about. I journaled about it, dreamed about it, plotted and planned with my girlfriends about who I could date the minute I turned sixteen. My inner life became, for several years, very one note.

One month after I turned sixteen, a tall boy with wide, brown eyes asked me out to the Dairy Queen.

"Can you pick me up after soccer practice?" I asked. He could. That day at our scrimmage, my friend Lindsay and I went for the ball at the same time. She won. I fell to the ground, rolling my ankle with a devastating *crack.* Black and blue, I hobbled to my potential beau's car after practice.

"You okay?" he asked. (I wasn't.)

"Yes!" I chirped. (My ankle was definitely broken.)

"If you say so," he said. "Maybe we can get you some ice?" (A wise suggestion.)

"No, thank you," I said, gritting my teeth. "I'm sure it's fine." (It would need surgery and take me out of sports for eight months, during which time my ice hockey team would win a state championship *without me*. But hey, at least I got to go to the Dairy Queen with a cute boy!)

Daryl and I have a preteen of our own now, with two more on the way, and we've started talking about how to help shepherd them through their first romantic forays.

"We probably shouldn't let them date until they're sixteen," I said. The unexamined life will continue on with the patterns of the past unchanged.

"I mean, I'm open to that, but can I ask why you'd like to approach their dating lives in that way?" Daryl inquired. Master of curious questions, my Daryl. His own parents had been decidedly hands-off when it came to managing his romantic relationships. In fact, I think he's still technically engaged to the girl he proposed to in kindergarten. We should probably have that annulled.

"Well, it's what my parents did with me," I said. He then asked how it had worked out. "Hmmm," I responded. "I mean, it probably wasn't the *best* policy."

"How about this," he said. "Why don't we have regular conversations with each of them rather than setting policies? Let's see where they are at, what support they need, and go from there." This adaptive flexibility floored me. What if we just kept conversations going with our kids and tailored our approach to their individual maturity and needs? How novel!

Our oldest son Lincoln's first school dance was at fifth-grade science camp. He came home reporting that everyone just jumped around a lot and he was bored by the whole thing. In sixth grade, when he brought home a flyer for his school's autumn dance, we asked if he'd like to go.

"Never," he said. "Never again. Not going to happen." He's only twelve and we have miles to go before we sleep. But also, leaning into the flexibility of watching and learning together rather than establishing rigid rules for young love has already borne good fruit and conversation. Rigidity is nearly always simpler, and sometimes we do lay down rules, as we have when it comes to when our children will be allowed to have phones of their own (ninth or tenth grade) and social media (Never! Just kidding! Sort of!). But when it comes to preparing for and adapting to fraught changes, flexibility—and its close companion, curiosity—is nearly always a friend.

While fresh water is incredibly important for most ecosystems, briny water has its own role to play. Nestled in a valley on the western edge of the Great Basin lies Mono Lake. Just outside Yosemite National Park, Mono Lake is an endorheic or terminal lake, meaning it has no outlet. Over time water flows in and then evaporates, resulting in very salty water that gets even saltier over time. It is so salty a person will float atop its waters—just like in the Dead Sea. No fish can live in Mono Lake. Very little plant life can survive. And yet, it is brimming with life.

Daryl and the kids and I pull the minivan into a gravel parking lot, Mono Lake's south viewing area. We've hiked quite a bit on this road trip and they've been troupers, but yesterday they discovered a skate park in town that allowed them to ride their razor scooters up crazy concrete ramps, and now that's all they want to do.

"We'll go again later," we say. "It'll still be there when we get back." I see their furrowed brows and remember how angry I used to feel when my parents would take away my *Babysitter's Club* books because I wasn't looking out the window even though we'd driven all the way to Gettysburg or Yellowstone or Zion National Park.

"You can read after we see the sights," they'd say, holding my books hostage. I promised myself then that I'd never keep my own kids from doing what they really wanted to do on vacation. It is *vacation* after all.

But here we are. I barely hold myself back from saying *we have a skate park at home.*

Spiky round scrub mottles the flat approach to the lake with doves flying to and fro overhead. As we near, tufa pop up from the ground, funky towers of calcium carbonate that formed from springs in the lakebed when the waters were higher. The tufa have been left stranded in the wake of its recession. We are 320 miles from Los Angeles, yet LA County takes water from wherever it can to slake the thirst of its millions. Today, Mono Lake is over a hundred and fifty feet lower than it was in 1958. The tufa look like children's sandcastles, the kind you make by dripping wet sand through your fingers.

"Whoa," says Felicity, glancing at them. They are whimsical and ominous, strong yet delicate.

A volunteer naturalist has a spotting scope set up on the shore. She points out an Osprey nest fifty yards into the near waters of the lake. The tufa stick up there too, providing perfect nesting platforms for raptor families.

"I can see their babies!" Felicity pipes up as I lift her up to the scope. Brewer's Blackbirds dot the shore, hopping from tufa to tufa and then down to the waterline and back up again, scolding us and one another.

"Look," the naturalist says, and takes a step toward the water. Immediately massive clouds of tiny flies rise to ankle level and then settle down again.

"EW!" all three of the kids shout in unison.

"But look again," she says. She walks parallel to the shore and the flies lift and settle, lift and settle by the hundreds. "They aren't interested in people. Try it."

They tentatively walk to the shoreline, startling a bit as the flies rise and fall, but soon at ease with the knowledge that the insects won't land on them or bite.

"Why are they like that?" Wilson asks.

"They're alkali flies," she tells us. "They spend their whole lives on this lake eating they algae. And all the birds"—here she gestures to the dozens upon dozens of California Gulls and Wilson's Phalaropes just a bit offshore—"like to eat them!"

The nesting Ospreys have to travel to nearby rivers and other lakes to fish, but Mono Lake provides a safe haven for them to raise their young. Other birds like Eared Grebe feast on the brine shrimp that dwell so thickly in the lake it's nearly impossible to dip in a cup without catching at least a few. More than three hundred species of birds live at or visit Mono Lake each year, including 30 percent of the world's Eared Grebes and 85 percent of its California Gulls. It's a primary migratory stop on the Pacific Flyway, a north–south band followed by many species of birds traveling back and forth from the Arctic, Alaska, and Canada to Central and South America or even Antarctica.

A bird I don't recognize hops from the scrub and poses in the middle of the trail. It looks similar to the California thrashers I see on my walks back home, but it's slightly smaller and its breast is streaked rather than solid. I consult my field guide.

"Sage Thrasher!" I tell Daryl. I'm mesmerized. Enchanted. I want to stay for a year. But kids have eaten all the snacks, drained their water bottles, and now they're turning on us.

"Can we go to the skate park now?"

I return alone at dawn the next day, pulling into a parking lot on the lake's northwest side. Before my feet hit the ground, I spy a large woodpecker sitting atop a snag at the road's edge. I train my binoculars—it's a Lewis's. Another lifer.

This shore is filled to bursting with Red-necked Phalaropes dabbling in the shallows. As I watch, they lift as one, flying thirty yards to the left and landing briefly before taking off again to return to their first patch. From the end of the boardwalk, I see Spotted Sandpipers, scores of California Gulls, dozens of Eared Grebes, another family of Osprey.

A couple of American Avocets delicately walk near the reeds, the stiletto heels of the bird world, elongated and chic, with slender bills that end in a delicate upturn. The lake is still and calm, its surface smooth as porcelain. I hear a Savannah Sparrow, a White-crowned Sparrow, and fifteen more Yellow Warblers whose call—*sweet, sweet, so-sweet!*—threatens to drown out the quieter birds. There is a pause and then I hear a Virginia Rail, shy, beautiful, and much more often heard than seen.

Most of my birding takes place in Southern California: Orange County, San Diego, Los Angeles. The biodiversity and pleasant weather there spoils me; it isn't unusual to spot thirty or even forty different species within an hour. But here in the desert flats of the Great Basin, on the shores of a lake too salty for fish to survive, I see more total birds than I've ever seen in one place.

Water need not be fresh or pristine to provide an opportunity for wildlife to flourish. Birds love sewage plants and parking lot puddles and retention ponds. Our salted oceans hold tens of thousands of unique species of fish, and in an alkaline lake in the middle of a desert surrounded by vast granite peaks, life thrives. In fact, Mono Lake is one of the most productive ecosystems in all of California.

Wherever there is water, life will find a way.

Water molecules are incredibly flexible. They can adapt to different forms—solid, liquid, gas—but they can also change their structure due to different pressure. Water is tasteless and odorless and nearly color-less, a universal solvent that can easily accept a wide array of other soluble substances. Unlike most other substances, it can act as both an acid or a base. Water is the most abundant compound on earth's surface and all life depends upon it. Most healthy humans can survive without food for several weeks, but only a handful of days without water. It cleanses, refreshes, nourishes, and brings joy.

It is a well-known child-raising fact that many cranky kids, when placed in water, lose their crankiness. Whether it's a bath, a lake, or a backyard sprinkler, nothing lifts the pall of a bad day like water. And this miraculous substance is happy to help, ready to serve.

But all good things must have their limits.

This far you may come and no farther, God says to the sea in the book of Job, and he says the same to us. We have limits. We are finite beings. The notion that God never gives us more than we can handle isn't actually in the Bible, despite common clichés to the contrary.

Yet the sea *does* sometimes exceed its bounds. I remember waking up on the day after Christmas in 2004 to learn that an earthquake in the Indian Ocean triggered a tsunami that killed over 200,000 people in fourteen different countries—170,000 of them in Indonesia's Aceh Province alone. Increasing water levels are washing away homes in North Carolina. Coastal erosion is causing landslides in California. The tiny Pacific island of Nauru is watching sea levels rise along its coast at a rate of 3mm per year, greater than the global average. At only 8.1 square miles, Nauru does not have many millimeters to cede to the sea before it will cease to exist.

When we are pushed past our limits, when change takes us beyond what we can manage or comprehend, when there is no more adaptation possible, what then?

When the prophet Elijah came to the end of himself, he said goodbye to his servant at the edge of a great wilderness to go ahead alone. Elijah had been serving God faithfully, courageously, consistently, and yet his reward was a fast pursuit by a bloodthirsty Ahab and Jezebel. He spoke up for God and now the king and queen would stop at nothing to see him dead. Debilitated and afraid, he walked on into the desert with no plan, no provisions, and no hope.

When he reached absolute exhaustion and despair, he laid down to rest, but there was no dignity even there. He could not find decent shade in this parched and arid landscape. Eventually he collapsed underneath a broom bush—small, prickly, scrubby. Discouraged and broken, he rested his weary body and prayed for death.

"*I have had enough, Lord,*" he said. "*Take my life.*"

Have you ever been pushed to this point of devastation, crying out to God for mercy in your anguish, bewildered that the one who promised never to leave you has yet to come through? We lionize figures in Scripture—Moses, David, Esther, Peter—yet they were each human, too, arriving at their own breaking points, pushed there by unexpected change. Only God is indefatigable. Infinite. Perfect. We have limits, physical and emotional, mental and spiritual—real points past which it is simply not possible for us to go.

In his despair, Elijah fell asleep—but only for a moment. The fine thread between life and death can also weave a miracle. Asleep in the wilderness, exposed, helpless, and alone, Elijah was awakened by one of God's messengers.

"Get up and eat," said the angel. Disoriented, Elijah looked around and discovered fresh bread and a jar of water. I love this detail. God doesn't make a bubbling spring appear from the ground. Instead, the angel comes with a jar, a container filled and prepared to make drinking easier. Elijah could have no doubt that the divine is at work. Springs can appear from thirsty ground, but jars in the wilderness? Bread? There's divine agency at work.

Elijah ate and drank and then laid back down and went back to sleep. But the angel wasn't finished.

"Get up and eat, for the journey is too much for you," the angel said, and Elijah woke to eat and drink some more. It is telling that the angel does not come to him with words of challenge. The angel didn't rally him to action, telling him to buck up, little camper *because God's people are overcomers!* No, instead the messenger came with a gentle offer of what Elijah's body and soul truly need most: a snack and a nap.

When we can go no further, God is there at the edge of what is possible, granting us rest. And when we are ready, often our first step back into the land of the living is to make sure we are rested—and watered.

Water is so adaptable in part because it always seeks the easiest route.

"Just put the bar down on the floor," my friend Kristy is fond of saying. "It makes it much easier to step over."

In times of change, we may need to give ourselves—and those around us—even more grace.

"Try less hard," Daryl tells me during the last days of the children's summer vacation. Our chore charts have come and gone. The house is a mess. Everyone is picking low-stakes fights with everyone else. Last night's dinner was—I kid you not—Popsicles, pepperoni, and chips with guacamole.

The kids are about to transition back into the school year in half a week, and they feel it. The incoming press of homework, the stress of new teachers, the fears about playground politics and whether or not that one mean kid we are praying has moved on will be in their class again. I've run fresh out of summer craft-and-idea magic, and they feel that too. The clock is ticking.

"Try less hard," Daryl says to me again, and I remember the gentle grace our God extends to us when we are facing tough transitions. Food and water in the wilderness. Rain to nourish the ground. Salty seas to keep us afloat.

Change is hard. Adaptation takes time. And sometimes we might even give ourselves permission to take the easiest path downstream.

I crack open the freezer and grab a colorful box.

"Grape or lime?" I ask the kids, and they cheer.

"Can we have pepperoni too?"

Resilience:

the ability to bounce back or carry on after a change or setback.

Resilience helps us arrive at a new healthy and stable place after a transition, particularly one that is difficult or painful. Think of the Bald Eagle or Brown Pelican populations that were decimated in the 1970s by the pesticide DDT. Both species of birds are quite large, and when DDT exposure resulted in weakened eggshells, their eggs would often break during incubation. After the chemical was banned, these bird populations rebounded. Today both eagles and pelicans thrive in large, healthy numbers.

Resilience assures us that change can be managed, recovered from, and sometimes even enjoyed.

15

Wind

So it is with everyone who is born of the Spirit.

JOHN 3:8

SO MUCH OF THE NATURAL WORLD goes about life unobserved. Some wonders are too remote or dangerous for us to reach. Others happen in hidden places—under the ground, at the bottom of the sea, inside our very own guts. Still others remain largely unnoticed even though they are all around us because they are too small to see with the naked eye. For example, plankton are small, sometimes even microscopically tiny organisms without the means to propel themselves. They are left at the mercy of currents and breezes. Integral to our planet's ecosystem, plankton have little agency within it. They're nomads, vagabonds, adventurers. Even the name plankton means drifter, coming from the Greek *planktos*, or wanderer.

Though we may most commonly think of plankton as creatures that live in water, there are miniature organisms that ride the currents of air as well. These breeze-driven insects, protists, fungi, arachnids, spores, and other microbes are called *aeroplankton*. They're up there at any given moment, swirling around us. This knowledge can lend an air of whimsy to even an everyday walk around the neighborhood—there is nearly invisible glitter, tiny bits of life shimmering all around. It can also lend an air of horror—some of those aeroplankton microbes are bacteria and viruses, most harmless, but a few very, very much not. Aeroplankton, small as they are, affect everything from weather patterns to global health.

Plankton live their lives adrift, going wherever the pull of water or wind requires. What a restful, hopeful, terrifying way to exist. There are times when we all must take a stand. When we mustn't simply follow the crowd or the current. But when the winds of change blow? Are we to fight them or to acquiesce? What if we aren't sure where they'll take us? Not all shifts should simply be accepted. Sometimes we must fight the winds of change or we'll reap the whirlwind. Other times, we can enjoy the ride. The key is discerning which is which.

Wind is the only one of the historic four elements that is invisible. We stand upon the earth, swim in the water, and warm ourselves by the fire, but the wind is a mysterious traveler. Barbara Mahany notes in *The Book of Nature*, "All we know of it comes to us secondhand; we only detect it by consequence: keeping watch on the quivering leaves, following the bounce of the tumbleweed across the dusty plain, catching the spit of the lake as it slices off top foam of waves." Like so much of the natural world, we tend to pay wind little attention until it affects us directly. When a candy wrapper blows out of my car and I have to chase it down in the parking lot, or the gusts are too loud for me to hear the birds, or the Santa Anas roll in to Southern California, it is then that I think of the wind.

Every autumn the southwestern United States begins to bake under a brutal sun. From late September into October, while the rest of the country is pulling on their sweaters and heading to the pumpkin patch or the apple orchard, here we face unrelenting, unyielding heat. Our hottest days of the year come after the calendar has turned to fall and the big box stores have stowed away their summer inventory to make space for scarves and coats and boots. The first year we lived in California, I tried to buy a new bathing suit in September only to be told that they were gone because they were *seasonal*. Back in the

Midwest the leaves will be turning and the chill descending; Alaska and Maine may even have their first dustings of snow. But in Southern California, our autumn begins with serious desert heat. And then come the winds.

According to the National Weather Service, Santa Ana winds occur "when air from a region of high pressure over the dry, desert region of the southwestern United States flows westward toward low pressure located off the California coast." Because the air gets compressed as it moves downward over the mountains, even cool evening desert air will heat up until it feels like something out of a blast furnace.

After a decade in Southern California, I have learned to dread the Santa Anas. They dry out our eyes and skin; they scorch our yards and parks. Everyone becomes just a little bit cranky, a bit more on edge. But the most ominous part is that where there is wind, there is often fire.

In the late morning of September 9, 2024, the Orange County Public Works was up in Trabuco Canyon conducting, ironically, fire prevention activities. A dropped boulder created a single spark and that spark hit a patch of dry brush. On a day with temperatures already rising above one-hundred degrees, a single spark was all it took. By early afternoon, neighborhoods surrounding the canyon—including several that held homes belonging to our congregants—were evacuated due to the roaring flames of the newly named Airport Fire. By the time it was extinguished on October 5 due to a combination of heroic effort of firefighters from around the country and a blessed drop in temperature, over 20,000 acres were burned, nineteen firefighters injured, and 160 structures destroyed.

The Santa Anas used to blow only in the fall, but now we face them much more frequently. The Airport Fire was fast-moving and destructive, but only a few months later and a few miles up the road in Los Angeles County, the Palisades and Eaton fires would burn over 57,000 acres and over 16,000 structures in mere days, again spurred on by the Santa Ana winds.

Wind is a powerful, fearful thing. It can destroy us with its fires, hurricanes, and tornadoes. It can blow cars off the freeway, roofs from our
houses, water past its bounds. Yet in its gentler guises, wind can be a
blessing and a joy. Breezes help cool us on sweltering days; friendly,
sustained gusts can allow us to fly kites and sail boats. It's the breath
of the earth, the force that helps spread seeds and aromas, rainclouds
and aeroplankton.

Often we find ourselves at the mercy of the wind, both the air
currents of our world and the wind of the Spirit. *The wind blows
wherever it pleases*, Jesus tells Nicodemus when the religious leader
visits him secretly in the dead of night. *You hear its sound, but you
cannot tell where it comes from or where it is going.* In Acts, the Spirit
alights on the disciples as tongues of flame, but only after the sound
of a violent rushing wind fills the house where they are staying. This
is no gentle breeze, no swirl of air that can be managed with a glider
or a sail. The Spirit comes in *power.* The wind blows where it will.

Yet the Holy Spirit does not come to destroy or consume but to draw
together. The power of the Spirit gives each of the disciples the ability
to speak in other languages, tongues they have not known. And they
go out, despite all the uncertainty and fear of those first tender days,
proclaiming the good news that Jesus has come, that hope is here, that
all will be well. The crowds, amazed, receive this news, as crowds so
often do, with astonishment, joy, and cynicism.

"They have had too much wine," say some, while others respond
with belief—and praise. This is the day of Pentecost—a day we celebrate in many of our modern churches by wearing red or decorating
with symbols of fire. A day of wind and flame, reminders that God did
not come as God-in-a-box or God-tame-and-placid. A reminder that
the divine is a force greater than any that shake and shape and batter
our world. A breeze, a spark, a raging, roaring wind. Fire to burn away

chaff, to open up the cones of the lodgepole pines, to cleanse the earth so that tiny, green shoots of new life can sprout once again.

Pentecost is a Big Deal Holiday in the Presbyterian Church. I didn't grow up Presbyterian, so dressing for Pentecost tends to elude me. Most years I forget to don anything crimson on the seventh Sunday after Easter. Half a decade ago, I was standing at the back of the sanctuary greeting newcomers and chatting with a beloved elderly woman when another congregant came over to gently chastise us both.

"You aren't wearing red!" the newcomer chirped, waving at our outfits.

"My undies are red," said the elderly woman without missing a beat.

"Ha!" said the congregant, heading back to her seat.

"They're not," said the elderly woman, leaning over to me with a grin. "But no one is going to check."

Laughter is another key to resilience. Our newcomer friend didn't know what this woman had endured: illness, injury, a loved one with a devastating diagnosis. She bore those changes with both lament and good humor, the sacred dance of what it means to be a human. We get knocked down. We rise again. And on a Pentecostal Sunday, we share a chuckle in the back of a sanctuary filled with the wild wind of the Holy Spirit.

In 2 Kings 2, Elijah is swept up to heaven in a whirlwind, riding in a chariot of fire. He's the only person in all of Scripture to whom this happens. Moses dies. David dies. Mary—the mother of Jesus himself—dies. We are told that Enoch walks with God and is no more, but even he receives no fiery transportation. Is Elijah's heavenly abduction a fluke or an example of divine license and creativity?

In Adam all die, writes Paul in 1 Corinthians, but not Elijah. Perhaps he is the exception that proves the rule, snatched upward because of divine favor or as an object lesson to Elisha, his prophet-in-training. Whatever the reason, Elijah escapes the only fate common to the rest of us. The Holy Spirit, that wind that blows where it will, swept God's prophet away. This is the same Spirit that alights in tongues of fire on the early disciples. The same Spirit that whispers to you and me today.

Pentecost shows us that there is no one-size-fits-all to the faith, translating the disciples' words into every tongue and language centuries after removing Elijah from this mortal coil. It's beautiful and telling in the story of Acts that the Spirit does not simply help every person present to understand the disciples' native Aramaic. Instead the Spirit translates their words so that everyone hears their words of good news in their native tongues. God-with-us. God-come-near. God-in-our-language.

God comes to each of us individually in guises we can receive, speaking a language we can understand. Sometimes there's an angel. Other times there are birds, oceans, a good friend, the proper book at the proper hour, or the cool wind that blows through at the moment of peak heat, bringing blessed, blessed relief.

"That's a God breeze," my friend Peg would tell me when she sensed the movement of the Spirit in a day off from the backbreaking work of cleaning houses. "God sends them when I need them most."

Perhaps one of the best questions we can ask when we face the winds of change is *who is behind them?* When the Spirit blows, even when the changes wrought will be uncomfortable or difficult, we can ride those currents with the wild abandon of the plankton, waiting and trusting to see where our good God will take us next.

Just above the southernmost tip of the globe, winds rage on unchecked by land. Once you travel south from the tip of Africa or New Zealand or South America, there are no longer any major land masses until you hit Antarctica, nothing but a sprinkling of small islands to interrupt the currents of air that spin their way around the earth. These perilous waters, known as the Drake Passage, are feared by pilots and seafarers

alike. Winds commonly get whipping up to 140 miles per hour—
Category 4 hurricane speed.

Humans struggle in such inhospitable conditions; this stretch of sea
is responsible for dozens, if not hundreds, of shipwrecks. Live to tell
the tale and you can buy a T-shirt that proudly proclaims, "I survived
the Drake Passage." But there are many, many animals that truly thrive
in those deadly waters and winds. It is a vital ecosystem for whales,
dolphins, seals, and hardy shorebirds like albatrosses, shags, skuas,
and petrels. Conditions that would shatter ships are a boon to these
tough, resilient creatures. Each of the animals that does well in the gale
has adapted by descending into the windless ocean or learning how to
use the whipping air currents for lift and distance. Wind—even a big,
bold wind—can work for us, if we let it. If we learn it. Standing up to
all the gusts life flings our way can capsize us, but learning to ride the
currents, practicing resiliency in the face of forces outside of our
control, steering rather than fighting, this can take us far.

This is the lesson of the plankton that sail where the currents take
them. For better or for worse, they live their lives at the mercy of wind
and wave. It is certainly a simpler way to live. When the change we
face is timely and necessary, or perhaps even just inevitable, we may
take our cue from the microbes that swirl and flow. Resilience requires
effort, and it's good to save our strength where we can.

"You can't fight the current," a whitewater instructor once yelled at
me over the roar of the Wolf River. "It will take you where it wants to
go. So keep your feet pointed downstream."

One of the seven wonders of the modern world, the Golden Gate
Bridge is a feat of engineering. Finished in 1937 by Joseph Strauss, an
engineer and poet, it spans nearly a mile and three quarters across San
Francisco Bay, connecting the city of San Francisco to Marin County
through its iconic International Orange beams and girders and abut-
ments. You may think that a structure like this, built on the windy bay,

would need to be rigid to withstand the elements. Yet the opposite is true: Its flex is what protects it from collapsing.

Leon Moisseiff, the engineer of New York City's Manhattan Bridge, was brought on as part of the Golden Gate team. He used the project to champion his "deflection theory" of suspension bridges. "The bridge would be lighter, longer, and narrower than any of its predecessors." The plan worked beautifully, and the Golden Gate was—and is—a grand success.

Buoyed by his new knowledge of wind and steel, Moisseiff then designed a bridge for Washington's Tacoma Narrows. "Galloping Gertie," as it was soon nicknamed, swayed fearfully in the northern gusts. Despite Moisseiff's calculations that it could withstand winds three times stronger, "it literally twisted itself apart in 42 mile-per-hour winds," collapsing completely on the morning of November 7, 1940. Thus ended Moisseiff's career.

Resilience can be defined as the ability to bend without breaking, to return after a setback, to take a disappointment and keep on going. A good bridge is resilient without being floppy, modeled in part after the silken strands of a spider's web that hold tension with a give. A bad bridge won't flex—or it will flex much too far. We, too, must find our equilibrium.

This spring our twelve-year-old son sat on the basketball bench as his favorite coach led his team to victory after victory. Lincoln had developed patellofemoral syndrome in his right knee and his orthopedist prescribed sports rest and twice-daily physical therapy for three weeks that then extended to six and then eight and then ten.

"Can I play on Saturday?" he'd beg his therapist as he performed exercise after painful, mundane exercise.

"It's not worth it, bud," AJ would tell him. "Not yet."

My mama's heart ached as I watched him sit on that bench. He went to practices just to hear the drills. He cheered on his teammates and honed his dribbling in a chair. Daryl and I grieved with him. We medicated his emotional pain with Chipotle burritos. We offered hugs and encouragement and empathy. We privately wondered how long we could survive in a house with an energetic twelve-year-old boy who wasn't allowed to run.

But even as we watched, Lincoln grew up. He developed newfound resilience. After complaining his way through week one of physical therapy—he hated the exercises, he hated the restrictions, he hated it *all*—he set his face to the task at hand and began working to heal. He became more compassionate toward friends with injuries and teammates who struggled. I watched the truth of the church fathers and mothers' assertions that one of the ways we grow up into Christian maturity is through suffering.

Resilience isn't sold anywhere; it is practiced, learned, earned. Often *hard* earned. And change can bring our greatest trials. Through it we are formed. Refined. Through its very difficulty, it can strengthen us. Hearten us for the journey ahead. As the author of Hebrews reminds us, *No discipline seems pleasant at the time, but painful. Later on, however, it produces a harvest of righteousness and peace for those who have been trained by it.*

God nurtures us through life's hard changes. The pruning we endure often strengthens us for greater challenges that lie ahead. While it can feel frightening to live life atop the winds that blow where they will, it helps me to remember who directs their paths. We are not at the mercy of a capricious universe or an uncaring God, aimlessly adrift. We walk hand in hand beside the one who promises to be, always and forever, God-with-us.

We do not sail alone.

16

Prairie

The hardest thing of all is to see what is really there.

J. A. BAKER

BACK IN 2014, a few months before I departed my Wisconsin pastorate for a new home in California, a mentor reached out to me. "When a pastor leaves a congregation that's been a mutually good fit, it's a little bit like parents mourning the death of a child," she told me. "Both parties are just too sad to comfort one another well." I took solace in this, as I had found my goodbyes stunted, stuck behind the wall of my own sorrow. I wanted to be fully present to each one, but the collective weight of grief had rubbed me raw. And I wasn't the only one feeling it. Over the previous days, a few of those within the church had pressed my hands and wished me well, but mostly they tucked notes of goodwill into my mailbox or else retreated into their own sadness and disappointment. Midwesterners tend to be people of few words and even fewer overt emotions. We'd rather skirt past sorrow than sit beside it.

But on my final Sunday, the pews were full. I felt the weight of this act of love. It was not without cost. That same pastor-friend was there to officially receive the congregational vote to "dissolve the relationship."

"I hate the term," she told me beforehand. As if the pastoral relationship was "made of salt or sugar instead of the Spirit."

I preached from the book of Jeremiah with its ancient reminders that God would be with each one of us wherever we went. Even in times of transition or grief we could take courage in and from this steadfast God. It was a steamy day, though still just early June, and many of us sweated through our clothes in the unairconditioned sanctuary. As I preached, I looked out through the stained-glass windows one final time, the sun streaming in, making colorful latticework on the red carpet and whitewashed pews.

After the service, I handed out cards with the central verse from the day's sermon and a personal word of love. People asked to hold Lincoln one more time, memories of his babyhood within these walls already fading, but it was past naptime. Lincoln was hot and surly and he repeatedly squirmed away.

"Will you post pictures of him sometimes?" an elder asked me, father to three boys of his own. "I had always . . ." he paused and swallowed hard. "I had always imagined I would get to see him grow up."

The disruptions wrought by change can leave us feeling bereft. It can be hard to see the good in something that leaves us shaken. Yet the natural world witnesses to the truth that sometimes it is the disruptions themselves that lead us to greater health.

"Prairie needs to be disturbed," my friend Dale tells me. He works for the Upper Mississippi Audubon as a conservation director and is often my phone-a-friend when I have birding or grassland questions. "If it doesn't get grazed or burned, it won't be healthy. In a similar way, it is the suffering that shapes us. We, too, grow the most from disturbance." He cited the example of wolves being reintroduced to the Midwestern ecosystem, bringing with them wild beauty but also significant death. But without the wolves, grazers overate the prairies, causing a decline in the native grasses and shrubs and then a corresponding decline of the insects, amphibians, reptiles, birds, and mammals that depended upon them. Wolves feed on grazers, and as the predator's population increased to a healthy level, the grazers' gradually decreased and then stabilized, giving the prairies just what they needed to thrive.

Disturbance can, paradoxically, keep us healthy. Resistance may be uncomfortable, but it can also build muscle, strength, and resilience. I know I'm not the only perimenopausal woman who has been told over and again that weight training will be a key not only to bone and muscle health but to physical stability and balance—essential for preventing falls—as I enter middle and then old age. Ease may feel cozy and good, but it can also be the enemy of wisdom and growth.

Consider it pure joy, my brothers and sisters, whenever you face trials of many kinds, writes James. I can perhaps see my way into patience or maybe even acceptance of these trials, but *joy?* That seems a bit far-fetched. Yet he continues, giving us the why. *Because the testing of your faith produces perseverance. Let perseverance finish its work so that you may be mature and complete, not lacking anything.* Maturity most often comes through struggle, not luxury or comfort. In order to grow, we must lean into change.

Every five hundred years or so, the church goes through a major time of upheaval. This began with its founding in the book of Acts, continued as Europe tipped into the Dark Ages, followed the Cistercian papal reformers in the eleventh and twelfth centuries, and ramped up again during the Protestant Reformation in 1517. The church, like the prairie, needs to be disturbed, particularly when it has gotten complacent, begun dabbling in affluence, or started trafficking in power.

Many religious scholars believe we are in the midst of another five-hundred-year shakeup, with trust in institutions at an all-time low, the rise of Christian nationalism and political populism, an epidemic of loneliness, and technological advancements that are vastly outpacing our ethics. I worry about this new shakeup in light of the dumbing down of so much rich theology in the church. So many people have given up deep biblical study for easy sound bites. So many follow charismatic leaders uncritically. I realize I may sound curmudgeonly here, but when we get the bulk of our spiritual teaching from social media influencers, podcasters, and shiny public speakers rather than the mothers and fathers of the church and a deep soak in the Scriptures—including their history, context, and languages—we are in for a very unpleasant ride. In an essay titled, "Christian Nationalism Is a Failure of Imagination," Karen Swallow Prior notes. "A flourishing Christian faith, along with a flourishing nation, depends on minds free and well-formed enough to recognize truth amid falsehood."

Knowing that we need to be stretched and tested, challenged and questioned and, yes, even occasionally disturbed, can help us attend to upheavals with courage rather than despair. It isn't that we will always be able to receive disturbance with joy—I appreciate James's invitation, but this will likely always be an uphill battle for most of us, myself included—but perhaps we can receive it with curiosity and patience, waiting to see its purposes in God's hands. This will help us build resilience, by God's grace.

Prairie plants grow very deep roots. According to the National Park Service, 75 to 80 percent of the biomass of these plants occurs below ground. The majority of prairie flora have roots that go down at least five feet into the soil with some—the compass plant and the cylindric blazing star, to name just two—descending up to *fifteen*.

In his *Sand County Almanac,* Aldo Leopold wrote of the compass plant, also called the Silphium. Wanting a sample of its sunflower-esque blooms for his own farmland, he became determined to transplant one from a nearby prairie.

"It was like digging an oak Sapling," he wrote. "After half an hour of hot grimy labor the root was still enlarging, like a great vertical sweet-potato. As far as I know, that Silphium root went clear through to bedrock." He soon gave up on his experiment and learned to enjoy the compass plant in its native habitat.

Prairie plants will face rain, snow, and wind, grazers that feed and trample, and even the occasional fire, but their roots sustain and hold them. Hardy sorts, many of them can survive anything short of a lengthy flood, ravaging tornado, or bulldozing human. Their root systems filter storm water, hold fast in high winds, and resist drought. They uphold them for decades, centuries, or even millennia. For prairie plants, roots are the key to resilience.

But even the strongest prairie plants cannot survive human destruction, noted Leopold. He observed the hardy Silphium plant at the mercy of landscapers. "For a few years my Silphium will try in vain to rise above the mowing machine, and then it will die. With it will die the prairie epoch." Resilient as it is, nature can be stressed too far. Overgrazing is as big a problem as under. If wolves cull too many deer, it will eventually result in their own starvation. We can all be pushed past the point of transformation and healthy change and into genuine crisis. Beyond resilience is not more resilience but rather collapse, combustion, extinction, despair.

Those on the margins are often quite resilient, but not because they are inherently strong (though they often are). It's because they've had no other choice. In an episode of *Life Kit Podcast* called, "Why you should stop complimenting people for being resilient," the host, "TK" Dutes, said, "Cancer patients are told they're so resilient and strong when they're just trying to live." On WWNO's *Sea Change*, New Orleans resident Carolyn Broussard put it this way, after surviving Hurricane Katrina: "I swear if I get called resilient one more time . . . I'm gonna scream." Difficult change has lasting effects, not all of them good. Hardship wears us down. Trauma can mark us forever.

Plus, putting the burden of bouncing back on those who have suffered—or even been harmed—can be a way of letting ourselves off the hook of loving our neighbors as ourselves and working for just systems in our world.

"This idea came up a lot," noted podcast host Carly Berlin. "That calling individual people resilient actually relieves responsibility from those in power to protect them from harm. . . . When people get called

resilient, what they actually hear is, 'Hey, sorry, you're on your own.'"
Often what those on the margins need most is not praise—*you're so
resilient!*—but practical care and systemic change.

Resilience is often a "have-to," not a "get-to." We become more resilient because there is no alternative. We become more resilient because the systems set in place by church or government or society to
protect us at our most vulnerable have failed. (Sometimes they've
never even been created in the first place.) We become more resilient
because the only other option is to cease existing.

A week after the birth of her son, I found the custodian of my Wisconsin church cleaning the sanctuary, her newborn in a bouncy seat,
her face pale and sweaty.

"Oh my goodness, why are you *here*?" I cried, setting down my
armful of hymnals.

"I couldn't miss the paycheck," she said, stooping to vacuum under
a pew.

"I am so sorry," I said. "We have failed you. Go home right now. I'll
finish. You will still receive that paycheck." I walked her and her baby
to their car with tears in my eyes. Just two months postpartum myself,
I'd been so caught up in negotiating my own parental leave and en-
during the rigors of pregnancy that I had forgotten to advocate for the
same for my own employee—and one whose job was much more
physically taxing than my own. How big our blind spots can be. How
often we only remember to tend to our own roots, forgetting that we
grow in a common soil together.

Am I my brother's keeper? Cain asks God, with disdain. The answer
has always been and will always be *yes*.

In Ephesians, Paul writes of our establishment in Christ, our connection to the deep source of all life. The key to Christian strength, to
congregational resilience, to personal peace is both the simplest and
the most mysterious of all things: love.

The First Nations Version translates Ephesians 3 in this way:

I pray that as you trust in him, your roots will go deep into the soil of his great love, and that from these roots you will draw the strength and courage needed to walk this sacred path together with all his holy people. This path of love is higher than the stars, deeper than the great waters, wider than the sky.

The NIV translates verse 17 as a reminder that we are *rooted and established in love*, that same deep, sweet potato-like root Aldo Leopold wrote about, not the thin filament roots of a shallow plant, easily torn from the earth. Prairie plants root all the way down to the water table, preserving them in times of drought, giving them nourishment even in the harshest of conditions.

This is Paul's invitation to us: to root down to love. The well is there, always there. Living water, life-giving grace. Life's storms and lacks will test our root systems time and time again. But God whispers through the porcupine grass and the stiff goldenrod, the smooth blue aster and the tall meadow rue—*drink deeply, dear ones*. A plant cannot make its roots grow any more than you or I can choose our height. What it can do is drink deeply of the nourishment it is offered. And as it does, God will make it grow.

I have learned to love and appreciate prairies even as I feel the ache of their struggle. Our prairies are not doing very well. Only a tragic 0.1 percent of Wisconsin's native prairie remains. That number is only slightly better or worse in nearby states: 4 percent in Kansas, 0.1 percent in Iowa. Illinois is a cautionary tale with only 0.01 percent of its native prairies still in existence with their precious, unbroken sod.

When the first European settlers arrived, 40 percent of what would become the United States was covered with grassland. Now we see it only in short, tattered fragments, many of which are threatened this very minute by development. The population of grassland birds has declined by 53 percent over the last 50 years, according to the American Bird Conservancy. Notes Rebecca Heiseman, this is "the greatest bird decline in any single terrestrial biome." No group of birds is doing particularly well, save for some species of gulls, pigeons, and the American Crows that have near-seamlessly adapted to urban and suburban environments. But prairie birds have been hit particularly hard due to habitat destruction, overgrazing, pollution, and climate change.

To sit with such news can feel like the end of the world. And yet, whenever I visit a prairie and watch the grasses and insects and birds so hard at work doing their God-given tasks, I can't help feeling the bittersweet pull of hope. The last scraps of prairie are somehow as moving and beautiful as the thousands of untouched miles of it used to be, even as they point toward its unimaginable devastation. They still speak. The birds keep singing. They remain as a witness of what was—and what still could be.

Human-wrought changes to the prairie have changed and shaped it. In many places, it's been annihilated. But the threats to our remaining prairie need not be fatal if we can hear and respond to the cries of the suffering. Dale sings the praises of bird-friendly beef, birding organizations partnering with local ranchers who have agreed to use sustainable grazing practices. Protecting ranchers' livelihoods, birds, and native plants are not mutually exclusive goals. For all to thrive, each must be taken into consideration and care. Healthy conservation pays attention to the needs of human animals too.

Closer to home, small, backyard changes like landscaping with native plants and using organic or bird-friendly pesticides can have an outsized effect on migratory grassland birds and the seeds and insects many of them like to eat. Every individual step is one step closer to collective flourishing. Often all the birds need is a little help to bounce back. Every mustard seed matters.

In Joshua 2, we meet a woman named Rahab. In true biblical fashion, no words are minced or euphemisms used. She is not an escort or a call girl or a lady of the night. She is introduced straight away as a prostitute.

Two Israelite spies enter Rahab's house. She takes them in, hides and protects them, and the town of Jericho gossips, as towns still do today. Word of her deed reaches the king.

"Bring out the men," he tells her via a messenger, but Rahab refuses to bow to an empire that has brought her nothing but pain and otheredness. Instead she hides the spies—saving them from near-certain death—and asks them for her own salvation in return. Rahab is an outsider, a survivor, no stranger to the scrappiness needed to make it through the day.

"The Lord your God is God," she tells the spies, recounting what her city has heard of the miraculous parting of the Red Sea and the victory over the kings of the Amorites. She asks for protection for her family— her mother and father and siblings, for Rahab has no husband or children. Her canniness opens her eyes to faith—and salvation.

The spies make good on their promise, and days later when Jericho falls, Rahab and her family are spared the same fate. The story concludes by telling us that she lives among the Israelites to that very day. Often resilience relies upon unlikely partnerships: wolves and prairie, courage and defiance, curiosity and adaptability.

Rahab's story doesn't end in the Israelite camp but hundreds of years later in the first chapter of Matthew. There we meet her not as prostitute but as the mother of Boaz, the great-great-grandmother of David, and the many-times-great-grandmother of Joseph, the father of Jesus. She has risen from a place of disrepute to one of greatest honor—a named ancestor of the Messiah, the King of kings.

God-given change can set us on better paths, those we never could have discovered on our own. When Rahab's city crumbles to dust, she and her family are not only spared but saved. This is not the ease of remaining at home, the familiarity of plying the tough trade she has learned so well. Rahab faces the discomfort acclimating to a new society, a new culture, even a new religion among the Israelites in their camp. She will join their nomadic journey across the wilderness as they draw ever closer to the Promised Land.

But this disturbance is also the start of putting down new, healthy roots.

It so often is.

17

Decomposition

When you light a candle, you also cast a shadow.

URSULA Le GUIN

IT IS A HARD TRUTH THAT change is rarely uncomplicated. A single one may set in motion a cascade of dominoes, a slew of other changes that come quickly and unexpectedly on its heels. For example, a fallen tree is never as straightforward as a fallen tree. After it topples to the ground, the hawk must find another perch from which to hunt. The migrating sparrow requires a new landmark to signal to her that she's arrived back home. The family of buntings in its nest suddenly has no protection from the eyeline of the owl. The death of a single tree will create room for some saplings but crush others beneath its heft. A thousand details follow its fall.

When a tree dies, in some ways it becomes more filled with life than it's ever been. Dead trees that remain standing become snags, hollowed out over time to host a myriad of cavity nesters and tree dwellers—woodpeckers, owls, squirrels, raccoons. Those that tip over onto the forest floor will slowly become welcomed as a part of that floor themselves. Fungi will take hold on a fallen tree, transversing a trunk with its weblike filaments, many too thin to be seen by the naked eye, each aiding in the delicate processes of decomposition. As they begin to break down the tree, microscopic bacteria also set to work, as do grubs and ants, termites, wood roaches, and millipedes, their tapered legs walking delicately over the fragile paths of decay.

What we see on the forest floor is at once holy and macabre. The cycles of our ecosystems invite and allow the bodies of the dead—the once-mighty oak, the powerful bear, the soaring eagle—to nourish the living. Pieces that remain after all the scavengers have done their work—bone, sinew, gristle—will eventually become the soil below. And here we are, people and plants and animals, building our lives upon and above those who have gone before us.

Unless a kernel of wheat falls to the ground and dies, it remains only a single seed, Jesus tells us. *But if it dies, it produces many seeds.* We can watch this in the understory, the mighty toppled oak making room, its own acorns sprouting up, its absence allowing light to reach previously dark places. It may even feed the next generation of oaks as it lays down to rest. Fallen trees that provide nourishment for seedlings are called "nurse logs." But there's a twist: *Anyone who loves their life will lose it,* Jesus continues, reminding us not to cling to what is fleeting.

This sentiment is woven throughout the gospel story, Christ's reminder to us to delight in creation—and in ourselves as a piece of the whole—but never seek to own or claim it. *Do not hold on to me,* Jesus tells Mary after his resurrection, gently asking her to release his healed, transformed body, signaling to us all that what is best and truest may also not be captured or pinned down. There is a wildness to Jesus, one that we see echoed in our forests and oceans and wetlands and deserts.

Change rarely comes without pain.

As we prepared to move from Wisconsin to California, Daryl listed our big, black drum composter for free on Craigslist. His pride and joy, the compost held within this drum was just on the verge of turning into rich, black soil. Daryl had babied our vegetable peelings, coffee grounds, eggshells, apple cores, and garden trimmings for several years, turning the drum on a careful schedule in order to ensure successful blending.

"Gotta go cook the garbage," he'd say, heading out in his flannel shirt, almost unrecognizable from the boy I'd married. The one who, during his first visit to my parents' house, didn't want to walk down to the lake because he might get his shoes dirty (you should have seen my sisters roll their eyes) was now *cooking the garbage.*

When he realized there was no way to move the composter to our new, yardless California condo, there were a few days of grief and then a turn to practicality. He wanted to make sure it would go to someone who could make use not only of the composter but of the soil that was only a few months away from perfection. He offered both as a package deal for free.

"Bring a truck," he wrote in the ad. "Whoever takes the drum must take the soil-in-progress also." There was immediate, widespread interest. He wrote back to the first people to contact him, holding several others in reserve. The first responders—a man and woman—agreed enthusiastically to take both the composter and its contents and thanked him for his generosity.

It'll work perfectly in our garden! they wrote, and scheduled a pick up for Sunday morning at 10:30 a.m.—right in the middle of our last worship service in Clinton.

When we walked out of the sanctuary around noon, sweaty and tearful, I held a handful of cards from congregants and a squirming Lincoln, eager to kick off my heels and release the flood of tears I'd been holding back only semi-successfully. Daryl held the side door of the church open for us. Our garden was just a few yards away, and as we carried our overtired boy across the lawn, we gasped. The people who came to pick up the composter had indeed taken it. But they'd scooped out all the compost and left it strewn all over the ground. Rotting banana peels, partially decomposed apple cores, moldering onion tops, and all manner of hot, stinky soil-to-be was scattered far and wide.

"Well, that's a disappointment," Daryl said finally. "Why don't you put Lincoln down for a nap while I get my gloves and clean this up."

It felt like a metaphor, but I couldn't decide for what. Were we not leaving our community better than we found it? Had we created a mess that others would be forced to pick up? Had we, too, made promises we wouldn't keep?

After helping Lincoln snuggle up with his stuffed jaguar for his final nap in a crib the movers would pick up early the next day, I stood at the window overlooking the garden, watched Daryl work, and let my tears flow. *Almost* fully decomposed compost is no good to anyone—it isn't yet soil. It can't be integrated into the ground without a good deal of smell and the attraction of flies and other pests. He bagged it up, stinky handful by stinky handful, slopping it into black trash bags before hauling them to the curb. There were too many bags to fit inside our can, so he pulled off his gloves, took his phone from his pocket, and sent a text. I suspected the message was for Marty, the Building and Grounds elder who would oversee the turnover of the church's manse that had been our home. We'd all said our goodbyes, but now the two of them would have one final interaction about garbage. I felt wrung out like a dishrag.

This is not how I wanted things to break down.

The process of decomposition can be quite unpleasant to the naked eye. In our kitchens, apples go mossy, carrots liquefy, and that forgotten hamburger patty in the back of the fridge begins to look like something out of a horror film. But peer a little more closely and there are wonders to be observed. Most organisms that aid in decomposition are teeny tiny, microscopic—bacteria and protozoa, a world of workers beyond our vision. Those that are big enough to see without magnification include some fungi and invertebrates like millipedes, maggots, termites, and the humble earthworm—the gentlest and friendliest of decomposers. The invertebrates who work to break down organic matter are sometimes called detritivores, one of those delightfully illustrative words the scientific community has gifted to us.

Each of these small natural wonders, from the microbes to the millipedes, sets diligently to its God-given task, disintegrating complex plant or animal matter into simpler substances—turning the body of an animal or the trunk of a tree into carbon dioxide, water, mineral salts, fructose, or glucose. Together they return what was once a living, breathing creature or a towering, mighty plant to the earth, bit by bit and day by day. It is a surprisingly orderly, even beautiful process. Decomposers depend upon death to do their work, and ecosystems depend upon the decomposers to avoid being overwhelmed with too much death all at once.

All of this takes time, of course. Days and weeks for the first stages, the leaching of water in plants, the cooling and bloat in animals, but then years—even decades—for something like that fallen tree or dead bear to be reabsorbed and redistributed into the environment completely. Scavengers and predators can help speed up the process. But it will still all take time. The rhythms of the natural world have reasons for their serene pacing, and they don't often respond well to being rushed.

Perhaps the most humorous example of trying to hurry a decomposing animal into obscurity comes from a sperm whale that washed ashore in Florence, Oregon, in November of 1970. Whales didn't often end up there, and for a few days the whale became a simple curiosity. Seeing a sperm whale up close is a wonder, even if it does happen to be no longer alive. But within a handful of days, the carcass began to smell and the city wanted it gone. They needed to come up with a plan to dispose of this multi-ton creature—and fast.

Notes Stuart Tomlinson in *The Oregonian*, "Burying was iffy because the waves would likely have just uncovered the carcass. It was too big to burn. So the plan was hatched: let's blow it up." A crew surrounded the unfortunate cetacean with twenty cases of dynamite, piling them around it on the shore side in hopes that most of the whale would explode in the direction of the water. A safety zone was cordoned off in every direction to protect a curious public. Then "at 3:45pm Thursday, November 12, the plunger was pushed."

Continues Tomlinson, "The whale blew up all right, but the ¼-mile safety zone wasn't quite large enough. Whale blubber and whale parts fell from the sky, smashing into cars and people. No one was hurt, but pretty much everyone was wearing whale bits and pieces." When the news report of this debacle was resurrected in 2013, including a video of the exploding whale, it became the sixth most-watched BBC special of the year.

The whole state of Oregon learned an important lesson that day about the graceful beauty of decomposition. Sure, a dead whale will smell, but at least you won't be wearing it.

Change transforms us. The illness we suffer can help us develop compassion. The new title broadens our shoulders with its increase in responsibilities. The seasons remind us to go up to the attic and bring down the winter coats and then, four or five months later, to pack them back into storage once again.

Even small changes leave their mark. But major, painful change can leave us gasping and grasping, feeling like we ourselves are the newly felled oak on the ground, about to be broken down into our component parts. Yet, as Lore Ferguson Wilbert notes in *The Understory*, "We do not grow by staying exactly the same."

Daryl's bout with the shingles virus turned him perpetually cold. Though he was fine during the day, suddenly he was shivering all night, even months and years after the disease had run its course. We bought him a heated blanket and a wool one to layer on top of that, a winter hat, layered long johns. (Perimenopausal me slept with just a top sheet and a directional fan and constantly awoke sweating.) No matter how many layers he wore, he woke up night after night gripped by a persistent icy chill, walking haggard through the long days that followed. I thought of Beth March in *Little Women* whose encounter with scarlet fever leaves her forever changed, her heart weakened.

Daryl's heart was strong and his physician gave him a clean bill of health, but the cold plagued him.

"I'm not as strong as I was," he told me. "I can tell that the virus left its mark on me." While we both felt the new ache of bodies in their fifth decade of life, this transformation chastened us. It is a humble thing to be taken down by a microbe, and humbler still to have the changes it wrought be permanent.

Yet in strange ways, this physical weakness became for us a conduit for God's faithfulness. As Christian Wiman notes, "The dark night of the soul . . . is an annihilating but necessary prelude to a renewed awareness of God." I awaken most days without Daryl. He has risen at four, driven from bed by the cold in his body, to walk the house (or the thankfully not-too-frigid Southern California streets) and pray, to light the fireplace in the living room or cocoon himself on the couch where he won't disturb me with his restlessness. He will be there to greet the children when they bundle out of their rooms at six, wrapped in blankets and robes, still fragrant with the perfume of sleep. For Daryl, a person who can be quite intimidating—six-foot-one with a full beard and a booming voice—this strange weakness has tethered him to the divine tenderness that meets him in the chill of the early silences. Christ is a companion to him in the loneliness of the predawn.

Before shingles, Daryl and I would nearly always greet the morning entwined, my head on his shoulder, his arm tucked around me, our bodies warmed by one another. These days I wake alone, putting an arm to my side, searching for his hand and met with nothing but air. It is a reminder of all those who labor while I sleep. The congregants who have shared with me their struggles with insomnia or grief, the workers on the night shift, those sleepless with worry or fear. Daryl's absence in our bed is a reminder to me to begin the day with prayer for those who suffer or labor unseen.

Our transformation from one thing to another—towering tree to nurse log, young firebrands to seasoned sages, invincible youths to nurturing elders—can be its own unique grace. This beautiful, painful process is written throughout God's good creation and into our own hearts too. There are wonders to behold on the other side of painful change. As Howard Thurman writes, "The old song of my spirit has wearied itself out. . . . I will sing a new song. Teach me, my Father, that I might learn with the abandonment and enthusiasm of Jesus, the fresh new accent, the untried melody, to meet the untried morrow."

Would the tree prefer to keep standing forever? I expect that it would. None of us chooses weakness. Few of us readily embrace the suffering of transformation. But there is grace even in the fall, if we will seek it.

Once during a homeschooling field trip, my mother brought my sisters and me to a nature conservancy where the topic of the day was soil. I arrived bored already, and doubly so since the boy I had a crush on wouldn't even be there. Our guide for the day was placid, bearded, and gently cheerful in the way so many nature-loving folks are. The first thing he had us do was take a few toothpicks, a ruler, and some string and cordon off one square foot of the forest floor apiece.

"Now look at it," he said. "Look really closely."

We did, dutifully kneeling down to the sandy gray soil of northern Wisconsin. It looked a lot like dirt. A lot like nothing.

One of the more courageous kids raised a hand to ask, "How long will we be doing this?"

"We'll be doing it until we all learn how to see," he said. "Keep looking."

Acquiescing to an afternoon of boredom, I knelt into a ball, putting my elbows on the ground and my chin in my hands. I wished I'd at least chosen a patch of soil with some *leaves* in it or something. But then, as I watched, I began to notice that the blank soil wasn't actually blank. Mine had a line of tiny red ants traversing from one side to the other. A pale pink rootlet popped out of the ground at a corner. There *were* leaves, tiny green ones no bigger than my pinky fingernail, growing on black stalks almost too thin to see. A spider half the size of a dime walked through, uninterested in the ants. A few translucent insect wings sat in the center, disconnected from whatever creature they once belonged to and almost invisible to my eye.

"Look at the soil itself," he said. "What do you notice?" I began to see that my soil wasn't just gray. It had flecks of gold and silver and bronze, copper and tan and darkest black. The dirt wasn't uniform, it was multicolored, each grain of a varying size and shape. There was a bit of bark in my square, and when I flipped it over with a fingernail, a beetle the size of a grain of rice frantically burrowed into the loam.

"The soil is alive," said the guide. "It is making sense of things that have died—leaves and insects and plants and animals. It is creating out of death. Decomposition is a wonder." Though these lessons were laid out there before me on that breezy Wisconsin day, it wasn't until thirty years later that I learned, listening to my gardener-friend Anna, that dirt and soil are not the same thing. Dirt is a subset of soil, but soil is composed of so much more: minerals, organic matter, water, even air.

In his book *The Unsettling of America*, Wendell Berry sings the praises of soil, noting that "soil is the great connector of our lives, the source and destination of all. It is the healer and restorer and resurrector, by which disease passes into health, age into youth, death into life. Without proper care for it we can have no community, because without proper care for it we can have no life." Berry is a master of helping us see to the natural, beating heart of the matter. For all our skyscrapers and vehicles, digital technology and medical innovation, we still depend upon the most elemental of things for not only our survival but our connectedness with one another, too. Soil is magic.

I came of age in the evangelicalism of the 1990s, a faith that felt often frightened of, hostile to, and threatened by science. Our living room table held copies of *Ex Nihilo*, the magazine from Answers in Genesis, a ministry dedicated to teaching about a literal seven-day creationism. We switched off the television when PBS's Nova talked about evolution or timelines spanning millions of years. The nature center was revered for a homeschool field trip but kept its distance from the church.

This bifurcation is not only harmful but unnecessary. The Book of Nature holds the same wonders that are written to us in Scripture, albeit in different guises and voices. While the Bible was never intended to be a science textbook, it preaches a deep reverence of and care for the natural world. And science isn't a threat to our faith: it's one of its greatest gifts.

According to Peter Harris, part of what motivated him to cofound A Rocha, a Christian conservation ministry, was that "even the limited awareness that we had of the world around was constantly affirmed by our relationship with God and by Scripture." Science likes its proofs and studies and hypotheses while Scripture breathes in poetry, story, history, and metaphor. This is good. We need both. They are conversation partners in how we understand and move about the world, teachers in what it means to be human, to worship, to live, to love, and to die. "To see beauty in new places," writes pastor Debbie Blue in *Consider the Birds,* "you don't have to trick yourself—you just dig around a little bit, pay closer attention, allow yourself to be opened."

Decomposition teaches us that transformation from what we are to what we will be can be painful. It can take a long, long time. Our faith reminds us that God comes prepared with a plan from seedling to nurse tree and back again. I'm not always good at trusting this, at seeing benevolence when what I feel is shaken like a snow globe and possibly cracked as well. But I am getting better at pressing my face to the soil, turning the rock over with the toe of my boot, and looking more closely, trusting that I will see tiny miracles at work both around and within me. The agency and the ownership there are not our own but God's. God promises faithfulness that extends to a thousand generations. So even amid the breakdown of change, if we look closely, we may find a fine, bright filament of hope.

18

Endings

To grow is to change, and to be perfect is to have changed often.

JOHN HENRY NEWMAN

THE BRIGHT DAY IN SPRING that Pongo arrived, I was making dinner when I heard Wilson call me to the back of the house.

"Mommy!" he said. "You *have* to see this bird! I've never seen one like it before!" I quickly turned down the burner under the pasta water. The kids have discovered that I will drop anything for a cool bird. Felicity often takes advantage of this to pull me from my work for a crow or a sparrow, a gentle request for my attention as much as my avian appreciation. It's hard being the youngest, after all. But Wilson only calls me when a bird is a rarity, so I made haste to the sliding glass door.

In the center of our backyard, plucking up sunflower seeds fallen from the feeder, was a bird bigger than a robin but smaller than a crow. Its body was thick and round, its head small, its feet and beak a vibrant, coral pink. But here is where things got interesting: it was spotted black and bright white like an avian Dalmatian. *I'd* never seen one like it before, either.

"What *is* that?" asked Wilson and I pulled a field guide from the shelf only to find no clear answer. The bird scratched and pecked in the middle of our yard like a chicken, a docile expression on its doe-eyed face. I snapped a few pictures of it with my phone for proof and memory.

"It looks like a pigeon," I said, noting its shape.

"But what about the colors?"

"That's what I'm trying to figure out," I said, turning to a birding app. I love the detective work of birding. My friend Keith calls it "solving small puzzles." Those puzzles are made all the more exciting because the puzzle itself might startle and fly away at any moment.

It turns out that Rock Pigeons, those commonest of gray, avian city dwellers, can come in white as well as a variety of spotted versions known as *pied*. It's uncommon but not rare. While I'd never seen a Rock Pigeon in our yard, I had observed a small flock of them at the grocery store a few blocks away. "Rock Pigeon!" I proclaimed, showing Wilson the info.

"Coolest pigeon I've ever seen," he said. "He looks like cookies and crème." When the rest of the family arrived home, we introduced them to our new backyard dweller, who was quickly christened Pongo, after the daddy dog in *101 Dalmatians*. When he came back every day for a week, the kids claimed him as their pet. I'll admit that his presence warmed my heart too.

"Morning, Pongo," I'd say, sipping my tea on the back patio.

"Evening, Pongo," Daryl would say, taking hamburger patties out to the grill. Despite being hawk bait with his bright coloring, Pongo spent a good half a year in our yard, placidly making happy pigeon sounds, cleaning up the seeds other birds dropped from the feeder, strutting and preening and leaving droppings all over our back wall.

Then one autumn day, I took my tea to the patio, and he was gone.

"He'll be back," the kids said, confidently.

"He might be back," Daryl and I said, less so.

We would never see him again.

When the Old Testament kings and patriarchs die, the Hebrew Scriptures mourn them by saying, *He rested with his ancestors*. It is appealing, in a way, this idea of endings, of death as rest. We grow weary.

Our days are long. But at the end of all the striving will be peace, wholeness, shalom. The Anglican prayerbook contains a liturgy that asks God for rest *when the fever of life is over*. How often life feels like a fever, rushing as we do from one thing to the next, frantic and harried, with never enough time in the day!

Yet it isn't just rest that is claimed. The patriarchs don't meet their end alone. They rest *together* with their ancestors. Even in death, there is community. It is a collective rest, as they join the peace and presence of those who have come before them. We will not be left on our own. We will rest *with*. Resilience is a multi-generational story.

Death is the final change, the one all our lives wind their way to sooner or later. In hospice circles it is common to have conversations about "a good death," asking gravely ill patients what it is that would help ease their transition from this life to the next. Topics that are tricky to bring up in polite society are the bread and butter of hospice, opportunities to make final plans, to say what has gone unsaid, to make amends, to end in peace.

I served as a hospice chaplain for a brief season before going into pastoral ministry, and I use the tools I gained there nearly every day. It can be such a relief to name things, even hard things, rather than ignore or deny them. I've watched many a congregant breathe a sigh of relief when it's clear they won't have to expend precious energy tiptoeing around the knowledge that their bodies are giving out. God grants us permission to speak of what *is*.

So much of our medical system is dedicated to denying human mortality. We treat to cure. This can, of course, be good—those who can get better should! But too often we continue addressing illnesses that won't improve, poking and prodding and medicating, in part because conversations about ending are so difficult to have. Plus, acknowledging the finitude of another person means beginning to come to terms with our own.

Many years ago I sat at an unresponsive man's ICU bedside. He was ninety-eight years old with terminal Stage IV cancer. I held his hand

and was midway through the Lord's Prayer when his son and daughter-in-law bustled into the room.

"Oh good, the chaplain," said the son. "Can we pray?"

"Of course," I said. "What would you like to speak to God about?"

"Well, that he'd get *better*, of course!" he said, gesturing to his father. I prayed as the son requested, but looking back, I wish I would have asked one gentle follow up question: *What would getting better look like?* Death is impossibly painful to accept, and yet eventually it will come for us all. In those moments of nearing a finale, will we pray that things would somehow revert to how they were, fighting against what will be? Or might we face this change, this grief, and these new realities, trusting that God will comfort those who remain and be the bridge for those who depart?

Keeping the end in sight can help us to live well now. It was not uncommon for medieval scholars to leave a sign of death—a skull, usually, or the symbol of a coffin or wilting flowers—on their writing desks. A *memento mori*—a reminder that one day they would die. I have a gopher's skull sitting on mine for the same reason. *You are a mist that appears for a little while and then vanishes,* Scripture reminds us. *All people are like grass.* While this may sound bleak, and perhaps even a little bit creepy, I've found that an unflinching gaze at the reality of my finitude grants a helpful perspective. We are so prone to triteness, to distraction, and to treating our time on earth as though it would go on forever. Facing the idea of our ending regularly, thoughtfully, and realistically can root us into the precious day right in front of us. This is the time we've been given. We are promised nothing more.

In his book, *After the Worst Day Ever*, chaplain Duane R. Bidwell describes his work with children facing terminal, end-stage renal disease and the surprising things they taught him about hope. While we adults tend to tether our hope to future possibilities—we *hope* we can go hiking tomorrow, or even we *have hope* because we believe that

Jesus will return one day—the children to which Bidwell ministered tended to have a decidedly different perspective.

"Strong bonds with parents and other caregivers help children develop a capacity to hope," wrote Bidwell. "This reality shifts from the future to the present." Present hope tethers its bearers to the people who nurture them. When all else is scary and uncertain, these children found hope in the love that surrounded them. *Now* hope.

Difficult changes of this nature—a chronic or terminal illness, the destruction of a home or a homeland, the final breath of a loved one—can be particularly devastating. Everything has changed, vital connections have ended, and it can seem as though *all* truly is lost, not just the people and things that actually were. And yet, as Bidwell communed with these children, he noticed that they experienced hope in abundance, which in turn led to greater resilience. Bidwell puts it this way: "Children's stories of hope suggest it doesn't happen 'inside' people but between them."

From my brief time working as a hospice chaplain and my current decade-and-a-half of pastoral experience with end-of-life care, I have noticed the pattern Bidwell describes, though not just between people. I've noticed this *now hope* in the connections we form with God—an observation he nods to in his chapter on spirit—and with the natural world as well. It's as if hope, especially on the brink of potentially devastating change, the rot and ruin and terror of the long night, is not about reaching forward in time but instead about being right here, together, in this moment, for as long as we are allowed.

We weren't sure when or how or even whether to mourn Pongo. I was near-certain a bird of prey or the neighborhood cat (keep your cats indoors!) had done him in, but there were other possibilities as well. Pigeons are flocking birds, for one thing. For a season, our regular backyard birds—House Finch, House Sparrow, Lesser Goldfinch—and our little family had been his only companions. But was it possible he had found more pigeon friends of his own and taken off to live behind the grocery store down the street? Felicity decided that this was a certainty.

"I'm so glad Pongo found his family," she told me one day out of the blue, nearly a year after Pongo's last day in our yard. Endings echo long after they have occurred. "I bet he is very happy now."

Not knowing how things ended or will end can be painful, but it can also be a form of grace. God does not reveal to us the day of our death, allowing us to exist within the mist, taking each hour as it comes. We don't know in advance the last time a child will hold our hand to cross the street, or a spouse will caress our cheek, or a neighbor will stop to chat at the mailbox. We are all so fragile. Things change so fast. But *not knowing* is how the animals live, how children thrive. *Now* time, present to the present, removes the anticipatory pain of change, allowing us to be all in, right where we are.

Consider how the wild flowers grow, Jesus tells us. *They do not labor or spin.* Resilience comes with practice, but it also comes with an acceptance that as much as we may plan and prepare, we won't ever have as much control as we'd like. Accepting the changes life brings to us by taking each day as it comes, is one more way we can find our footing amidst seas of change. It is our Savior who reminds us that *each day will have enough trouble of its own.* This is true on the day of our birth. It will be true on the day of our ending, and it is true of all the days in between.

Autumn in Wisconsin is a season of extravagance and foreboding. The leaves turn colors vivid as fire, orange oaks and red maples and brilliant ocher aspen and birch. The slanting sun illuminates them until the forests glow like jewels, the throne room of heaven. And moving through it all is the icy breeze of change, stirring the leaves, cooling the ground, reminding us that winter is not far off. Within weeks or days or hours, winter will wrap the earth in its snow shroud and things will be dark and cold for a long, long time to come.

The years I pastored in southern Wisconsin, Daryl began to suffer from seasonal affective disorder, so we bought a little sun lamp to sit at his writing desk. He would gaze into it, hoping for relief. It helped a little. Making it through the bitter months is all about finding those things that help *a little* and then combining them into enough layers to survive. A wool blanket. A Florida orange. A trip to the local hotel's sauna to drive the chill from deep within the bones.

"I'm not ready for it to end," he would say as the last days of summer dropped away. My mother, too, always mourns the end of the warmer months. I remember watching her when I was a child. She'd hold her cup of coffee with both hands and stand near the picture window, sighing a sigh that seemed to come all the way from her toes.

"That's it then," she would say, her words as mournful as if she spoke of the death of a friend. "That's it for summer."

There is grief in the ending. Always grief. And yet there is a cleanness to ending, too, the delineation of seasons and habitats and days and years. Now that I reside in Southern California with its muted seasons, part of me misses the clarity of winter, the way it drove us to ache for the resurrection of spring. Blueberries taste better when you've waited nine months for them. Easter feels like Easter when the first crocuses are breaking through the crust of ice to sing their joy. In a place without real endings—here deciduous trees lazily lose their leaves in mid-January and bud again in March—how will we know when we've begun again?

When I am near the end of a big project, I cannot wait for it to be done. While I begin most endeavors with enthusiasm and energy, there comes a point where I become the horse headed to the barn. Head down, singularly focused, ready for home.

In my mid-thirties, I watched as Daryl and several of our friends came to the end of hard-earned PhDs in theology or New Testament. After years of focus-bordering-on-anguish, long nights and library runs and learning modern and ancient languages, feeling guilty whenever they *weren't* studying, living hand-to-mouth on stipends that were definitely *not* salaries, they finally came to the finish line. With the conclusions of their programs came celebrations and euphoria—for about three days. Then a creeping sense of lostness arrived, almost a feeling of grief.

"I have no idea what I might like to do for a hobby," my friend Chris told me. "All my time was dedicated to this degree." While other people developed leisure pursuits, Chris and Daryl and our other PhD-bound friends had next to no free time at all for years. What was a person to do when their singular pursuit had ended? Who were they to be?

I feel an echo of this loss when the kids are off visiting their grandparents. On the average day, all I want is a moment's peace, but when I finally have it, I don't feel peace but loss. The house is too big. The rooms too quiet. And then our brood comes home a day or two later, barreling into the house with their pillows and stuffed animals and duffle bags filled with dirty clothes and by bedtime I would do almost anything for a moment's peace again. Life is so funny that way. How many of our longings wouldn't satisfy us for more than a moment if they were fulfilled?

Whether basketball season has ended or retirement has arrived, the kids have moved out or the remodel is finished, endings can be rocky. We find ourselves with too much time or space, too few parameters on what we will do next. Endings are at least as difficult as beginnings. And then there is the unbearable pain of final endings—the last time we give the preschooler a bath because tomorrow she will prefer to do it herself, the final school concert for our lanky senior violinist, the summer camp that closes, the retirement from a job we loved. The unthinkable death of a family member or a friend that leaves us feeling unmoored forever.

If resilience is all about bouncing back, how might we practice it if the project or person or job or way of being is no longer there to bounce back *to*? I think of Jesus standing at Lazarus's tomb, Mary and

Martha devastated at the death of their brother. Jesus will resurrect this dead man. In moments Lazarus will walk out of the tomb trailing graveclothes behind him. But at this ending of death, this rift in the fabric of the cosmos, this deep and burning loss, Jesus weeps.

Ending well is no easy task. Finality is one of the hardest parts of change. We want to promise to stay in touch, to visit often, to recreate the closeness of the childhood friendship that's faded with distance and time. But many endings must simply be received and grieved. Clinging to what used to be will prevent us from growing into the change to which God calls us.

But here's a bit of good news: grief and peace aren't strangers but close cousins. As we mourn the change of endings, we will find God there. Writes Paul J. Pastor in *The Listening Day*, "Peace is the active rest of perfect trust, the solace of surrender."

So much of what we've learned about change comes down to this courageous act. Living with open hands before God, receiving both grace and pain, hope and hardship. And learning to trust the grand story that started long before us and will continue into the eternity that lies beyond. We witness this peace in the wild things that do not ask how or why. They simply *are*.

"They enjoy a seamless presence—a lyrical unity with the earth," wrote John O'Donohue.

Endings are painful, but they are also essential. Sometimes they can even be good. At some point in the autumn chill, the last mosquito dies. After a long night, the darkness ends and the sun begins to rise. Beyond our earthly conclusion we hope in a promised eternity where there will be no more *death or mourning or crying or pain,* for the old order of things will have passed away. All good things must come to an end, the saying goes, but all bad things will end one day too.

And when they do, even more goodness will open up beyond.

Wonder

*The world will always be beautiful
to those who look for beauty.*

MARGARET RENKL

J. A. BAKER WROTE his classic study of two Peregrine Falcons back in 1967. These falcons, the fastest birds on earth, are profoundly adept hunters. Baker follows them over the course of about six months, from fall until spring. After months with the falcons, Baker writes,

> He was not afraid, nor was he disturbed when I lowered and raised my binoculars or shifted my position. He was either indifferent or mildly curious. I think he regards me now as part hawk, part man; worth flying over to look at from time to time, but never wholly to be trusted; a crippled hawk, perhaps.

Baker's short, journal-style nonfiction makes for an engaging read, particularly for those of us who are birding enthusiasts. But what caught me in my current reading was the foreword by the writer Robert Macfarlane. Notes Macfarlane,

> [Baker] wrote *The Peregrine* following the diagnosis of a serious illness. This is never declared outright in the book, but it is nevertheless made clear that the narrator is suffering from some

deep wound, mental or physical, which tinges his perception with "dimness" and "desolation," as well as sharpening his awareness of beauty.

I don't know that Baker could have written *The Peregrine*, or at least could not have written it in the same soulful way, without his ailment. Vulnerability shifts our gaze in a way that few other things can.

This is the challenging truth of change: It will upend everything. It will break our hearts and eventually our bodies too. It will wake us up in the middle of the night like an owl haunting the alley. It will come unbidden, stay too long, and vanish without apology. Change can be unyielding, unwelcome, terrifying, and brutal. But change can also sharpen our awareness. It can teach us how to see.

Do you have eyes but fail to see, and ears but fail to hear? Jesus asks his disciples when they've too quickly moved on from the miracle of the loaves and fishes to grumble about what they'll eat for dinner. *Don't you remember?* Change can shake us awake to the work of God in the world, in our hearts and lives, in our neighborhoods and out in nature, too. Change—even hard, brutal change—can be a doorway into wonder.

A few days before Christmas in 2014, newly arrived in California, I contacted a woman online about buying a train set for our toddler son, Lincoln. Money was tighter-than-tight. Daryl was finishing his PhD, we were eating through our savings just to pay rent, and the steep cost of childcare prohibited me from finding additional part-time work. While the church was paying us more than fairly for the single salary we shared as co-pastors, surviving in an area with such high cost of living on one paycheck was not for the faint of heart. We were living hand-to-mouth. I found comfort and solidarity in Kate Bowler's reminiscence about when she and her husband were "not poor like sweet church mice. Poor like people who worried we would get scurvy because we couldn't afford to buy oranges."

Lincoln, then a newly minted two-year-old, would likely have been thrilled by receiving just a cardboard box and a trip to the park for Christmas, but I wanted him to have a train. *Thomas and Friends* was on repeat in our home, and he'd fallen hard for the gentle, British storytelling of James and Percy and Thomas and their adventures in being *really useful engines.* When I discovered a train table for five dollars at a garage sale—pre-scribbled on one side with crayon, but solid and sturdy enough, so we could just turn its ugly side to the wall—I became determined to hunt down trains to go with it.

I found a woman selling a massive used set—coal chutes, Tidmouth Sheds, a magnetic crane ("Cranky," of course), and extensive tracks that included hills and roundabouts. It was all fantastic and perfect and decidedly out of our budget.

"Is there any chance you'd be willing to part with just a few of the main trains and one circular track?" I asked, naming a much lower price and saying a silent prayer. She was. After I tucked Lincoln in bed, I drove over to her neighborhood just a mile or so from my own. I was surprised to discover that she was living in a condo just as small as ours, and I immediately felt extra gratitude toward her for being willing to sell only part of the set. No doubt she was trying to pull together enough money for Christmas gifts for her own brood.

I rang her doorbell, my carefully scrounged cash readied in my hand. She came to the door with the promised engines and tracks in a plastic bag, giving me a moment to make sure all was in order.

"Thank you so much," I told her, holding out her payment. She paused for a moment, and I could see her sizing me up, frazzled mom to frazzled mom. She glanced behind me and saw my old car. She looked back at me. It was not *not* obvious that I cut my own hair.

"Just a second," she said, and disappeared back inside, leaving me holding both the trains and my cash there on her front steps. She returned in a moment with three more bags of trains and tracks—the entire remainder of the set.

"Oh, thank you," I stammered, "but I can't really—" The hardest thing about being poor was having no money. The second hardest was trying to find ways to graciously cover over that fact. *No, thank you, I am not going to buy those jeans even though they're on sale and my old pair is threadbare. No, I didn't bid on the silent auction. No, let's not split the check evenly, because your burger was three dollars more than mine.* The woman stopped me and looked me straight in the eye.

"I know," she said. "Merry Christmas." She traded me the three additional bags of trains—tracks and stations and more engines than I knew existed in the Thomas Universe—for the few dollars I was holding out, gave me a smile, and returned inside. I stood on her porch for more than a moment, stunned by her generosity.

While creation is often the shortest distance between ache and delight, we must not forget that people are part of God's plan for care, provision, and tenderness too. We can help each other in the difficult process of weathering change. God has given us each other.

For all my love of the natural world, I do not believe that creation itself is inherently benevolent. Only God is all loving and all knowing. Nature is spectacular, provoking us to awe and delight, and it is also brutal and uncaring, *red*, as the old saying goes, *in tooth and claw*. Hurricanes arrive without a thought for the unhoused, the destitute. Parasitic animals make their lives by draining away the lives of others. Look up kudzu or Japanese knotweed or English ivy and never sleep again. Beauty and goodness are not synonymous—the same gorgeous vista that inspires us one day could kill us with an avalanche the next.

Yet I do believe, like Flannery O'Connor wrote of her beloved American South, that creation is "Christ-haunted." The Spirit hovers over the waters then as now, even when there is still darkness over the face of the deep. "Beauty is its own excuse for being," writes Kent Gramm in *Nature's Bible*. "Whenever I question myself, I remember that."

As we walk the hard road of change, chosen and unchosen, we can cling to that old American cliché that what doesn't kill us makes us stronger, but we also all know in our bones that this simply isn't true. Plenty of us, like Jacob of old, have wrestled with God and will now walk with a limp for the rest of our lives. We wear the pain of difficult changes in the lines around our eyes, the stoop in our shoulders, a waistline thickened by comfort foods, and yes, even that limp. None of this is easy.

We can see that sometimes rocks weather into beautiful formations—arches and canyons, or striated, colored cliffs. But also that eventually even what was once most majestic will crumble into dust. *The earth will wear out*, the book of Hebrews reminds us. We will too.

But in a world of quick fixes and easy answers, nature invites us into a deeper, slower rhythm of stasis and change, growth and assimilation, pruning and healing. These rhythms take time. They cannot be hurried. Ralph Waldo Emerson is believed to have called us to "adopt the pace of nature: her secret is patience." And herein lie the invitations of God to be still, to drink deeply, and to find our rest.

This is our final lesson—that wonder can do what all our preparation and good practices can't. And this is our final gift—that God will continue to orchestrate our encounters with wonder all the days of our lives. The gifts of awe and delight can move, hearten, and strengthen us when all our own best efforts have come up short. When our preparation, curiosity, adaptation, and resilience have taken us as far as they can. When we are burdened with change, confused by transition, or simply so tired of pivoting we don't think we can go on, God invites us to look up. Simply heading outside can be the beginning of how we find the path back home. As Robin Wall Kimmerer wrote in *Braiding Sweetgrass,* "The land knows you, even when you are lost."

At this year's San Diego Bird Festival, I get on a bus with fifty other birders to look for rarities along the US-Mexico border. It is an embarrassingly beautiful day for February, the skies blue and bright, the temperatures in the mid-sixties. Days like this are why people move to California. Our first stops yield two Ridgeways Rails, elusive, rarely seen marsh birds. We are a jovial bunch as we get back on the bus for our next stop—the Tijuana River Valley's Goat Canyon.

Now the weather turns on us, suddenly hot and oppressively windy. As we hike the trail to the border wall, that specter of separation and brutality, sand blows into our eyes and mouths and ears. My hat sails off into the chaparral, and I retrieve it, brushing off spiky twigs. The early morning's wonder has been replaced with grit between my teeth and a sunburn I can already feel developing on the back of my neck. We fall silent as one, keening our ears to listen, but none of us can hear a single bird call. The wind is roaring now. We trek on.

Around the bend, I stand between the two guides, my binoculars poised. This is the spot where they found an endangered California Gnatcatcher just days ago when they came to scout out the trail. Just up the ridge and beyond the wall, traffic pounds down Mexico's Federal Highway 1D.

"Let's wait just one more minute," one guide says. The birders around me shift their weight. The heat blasts. The semi trucks rumble past us just up the hill and beyond the wall. The wind is a gale. And then, out of nowhere, it stops. We descend into ethereal stillness. All is quiet.

In that tiny sanctuary in time, a small gray bird flies over us and alights on a chain link fence above a sign warning us not to trespass. It is the gnatcatcher. Temperamentally reclusive, this one stares at us from an open fence for one long moment. All around me camera shutters click. The bird wheezes its scolding call, cocks a bright black eye at us, and then vanishes back into the brush.

Then we hear the crunch of gravel beneath tires. It's the Border Patrol.

"You need to move on," a uniformed man tells us. "It's time to go." Here is the strange juxtaposition we so often find when it comes to wonder. Wonder sits right up against the ordinary, the strange, the unsettling, or even the unjust. An endangered bird atop an ugly fence. A moment of transcendent beauty occurs below a wall meant to separate one people from another. A break in the wind is all the more noticeable because of the painful, sandy gusts that came just before. As the poet Anton Wildgans once wrote, "What is to give light must endure burning."

I have a friend who took up jogging during a particularly painful transition in her life. Every morning she'd hit the road with Psalm 23 on her mind, timing its words to her footfalls.

"Sure-ly good-ness and mer-cy will fol-low me," she would recite, running out her anger, her angst, her sorrow.

"What is that lurking behind me?" she asked. "Not despair. Not judgment or criticism or fear. *Goodness. Mercy.*"

Weathering change is rarely easy. We will face challenges beyond what any of us would choose. Yet we keep going. Though the day is hot and windy, the sand blasting and the trail steep, the goodness of God marks our steps. We will see wonders if we keep looking up.

All the days of our lives we are held by this same God, this Good Shepherd. Change will come. Tough transitions are inevitable. And we will see the wonders of God.

It is spring again. Migration season. Nesting and then fledging season. A time of near-constant transitions, big and bold. The school year is winding down. The church is preparing for the bustle of summer camps and beach days and vacation Bible school. We're packing away coats and bringing out shorts and sundresses.

All around, things are being made new. Our nectarine trees are blossoming, their blooms fanning out like pink petticoats. The lavender and rosemary are attracting bees with their purple flowers. I suspect we have an Anna's Hummingbird pair nesting in the neighbor's tree that overhangs our barbecue, but I haven't yet been able to spot it. The parents scold me whenever I step too near.

In the other three seasons, wonder is a little more circumspect. The beauty is there, but it's subtler, more seasoned. Here in spring, it jumps up and down, waving its arms, shouting, "Look here! Don't miss it!" Even the most jaded among us can't help but notice. This spring it is the smells that have my attention: orange blossom and jasmine, so fresh and floral and alive that they stop me in my tracks. Even the breath of spring is a gift.

The Western fence lizards that make their home in our yard are cocky little things, just a few inches long. They do push-ups in the grass and on the sidewalk for reasons scientists still don't fully understand. They run up and down our stone wall all day in search of insects, clinging to it like Spider-Man with their sticky feet. They change colors to help them thermoregulate, going from light gray or tan to nearly black to soak up the sun. Occasionally one makes its way into our house and we have to perform a bumbling catch-and-release ritual straight out of a Laurel and Hardy film. They're harmless neighbors and we are glad to have them near.

A few years back, the kids and I were on a hike with friends when we spotted one of these common, everyday lizards looking astonishing. Rather than its usual drab camouflage, it sported bold greens and blues, the colors rippling and changing before our eyes like a Las Vegas sign. We circled it, aghast. Within a few seconds, a second lizard, this one more subtly colored, scooted out from the underbrush and met up with the first.

"Piggyback ride!" chirped one of the kids who was too young to have had The Talk yet. I knew male birds dressed in their finest for breeding season, but had no idea that our lizards did too. Just an ordinary day. Just an ordinary hike. And right there at our feet, magic.

And here is the wonder of God's good creation: we haven't even begun to scratch the surface. We will never arrive. Not in our own growth, not in our intimacy with Christ, not in our understanding of the marvels and miracles of the natural world. There are depths beyond depths still to be mined. Our transformation continues.

There is great hope in the hard knowledge that change is our story. We ache with it and yet it buoys us, too, as this strange dance of life carries us onward.

"Joy is at the end of it after all," Buechner tells us. "Astonishment and joy are what our faith finally points to."

I still struggle with change. I suspect now that I always will. But I am learning to face it with a newfound courage born from days with the birds and the wind, the ocean and the lizards, the prairie and forest and Mobula Rays and microscopic fungi. There is a purpose to the shaping of seasons and the speech of trees. If the earth is the Lord's then I, too, belong.

That doesn't make change easy. But it does make it interesting and amazing and ultimately very, very good.

Let us look to the birds, to the water and wind, to the forest, to the tiny particles of soil and the towering mountains and the last scraps of undisturbed prairie. Let us look into the eyes of our very own neighbors, one more piece of a beautiful whole. And here, in this wild, breathing, throbbing world, let us keep our eyes open for the Spirit of God, trusting that the God who goes before us will see us through this next change, too, whatever it may be.

Acknowledgments

To the wonderful folks at InterVarsity Press: Kelli Trujillo, Lori Neff, Cindy Bunch, Ted Olsen, Allie Noble, Terumi Echols, Krista Clayton, Jeanna Wiggins, Collin Huber, Ryan Mueller, and many more. I love working with each and every one of you. Thanks for taking on this project.

To my agent, Keely Boeving, who gets it, gets me, and gets the industry in ways that continue to blow my mind. You're the best.

To Presbyterian Church of the Master, each pastor, staff member, elder, deacon, volunteer, and congregant: Gosh, I'm so grateful for you and for what Jesus is inviting us to build together.

To my Ellis and Belcher families, for holding space for the strangeness that it is to have a writer in your midst. I love you all to the moon.

To my literary community: Laura, Karen, Liz, Cara, Seth, Will, Elliott, Beth, Sarah, Emily, Bethany, Nicole, Catherine, Amy, Roger, Glenys, Annette, Susie, Shawn, Maile, Margaret, Prasanta, Debbie, Yolanda, Duane, Kenn, Ted, Mary, Annie, Marlena, Kent, Jill, Lore, and Brian. Your words continue to push and inspire me.

To Dale Gentry for chatting with me about the beauty of prairies, and for answering all my woodpecker questions.

To my beta reader friends, Steve Kamm and Aarik Danielsen, who took on the labor of love that it is to read a full-length manuscript that's not quite there yet and then the courageous work of telling hard truths. I can't thank you both enough.

To Anna, Sonia, Del, and Hannah, for your near-daily conversations of friendship. My life is so much richer because you are in it.

To Lincoln, Wilson, and Felicity, who have my whole heart. You continue to teach me that the bittersweet nature of change is part of God's grand story.

And to Daryl, always my first reader and always my dearest love.

Questions for Reflection and Discussion

1. TOUGH TRANSITIONS

- Courtney begins the book with a story about a disappointing change in plans when she injured her foot before a family vacation. Can you think of a time when you faced an unexpected change? What do you remember about it?
- What is one small change you have faced in your life recently?
- What is one difficult change you are facing currently?
- Courtney lists two powerful guides we have when it comes to weathering change: God (revealed through Scripture, Jesus, and the Holy Spirit) and the Book of Nature—the good creation God sets before us. Have you ever experienced nature as a balm during times of difficult change? Share the story.

An invitation to action: Go outside for at least ten minutes one day this week. Look around. Journal or write down everything you notice with your senses of smell, hearing, sight, and touch. What do you notice about yourself as you quietly observe the natural world?

2. STASIS

- Stasis can be a time of stability and preparation, a season of peace and rest. Are you in a season of stasis right now? Why do you answer the way that you do?

- The psalmist invites us to "be still," a way of understanding and acknowledging that God is God (and we are not!). Do you find it difficult or easy to be still?

- Courtney writes that Monarch caterpillars don't just grow wings and turn into butterflies: first they must spin a chrysalis and then dissolve into goo! Transitions can feel this confusing and scary for us too. Have you ever felt completely unmade and remade by a big life change?

- *Torpor* is a sleep-like state that many birds and animals use to conserve energy, especially at night. What have you found that helps you conserve energy, particularly in seasons of difficult change?

An invitation to action: Set a timer for ten minutes, sit outside or near a window, and be still in the presence of God. It may help you to look for birds or insects as part of your stillness practice.

3. FORESTS

- Do you agree with Courtney that "forests have a smell"? What do you think about when you remember the smell of a forest?

- Courtney writes that trees bud at the end of autumn, their tender future flowers and branches protected throughout the winter's chill by "sleeping-bag-like structures" that keep them warm. Trees are an illustration of how we might prepare for the changes ahead—the pause of winter and then the colorful explosion of spring, for example. In what ways are you preparing for change today?

- Change is our lot in life, yet Scripture teaches that Jesus is the same "yesterday, today, and forever." How does it shape your faith to know that we worship a God who never changes?

- Are you close to retirement, already retired, or far from it? What comes to mind when you think about the final span of your life?

An invitation to action: Go out to a forest this week. Smell the smells. Turn over a dead log or two and examine what you see there. Count the leaves. Watch the birds. Find your footing. Listen deeply: Do you hear anything from God?

4. FLEDGING

- Courtney writes the story of watching a fledgling House Finch struggle to feed herself. The bird's father both cares and seems exasperated at her reluctance to learn this lifesaving skill. Can you think of the last time you learned something new? How did you feel at first?

- How did you feel after you'd learned that new skill?

- Courtney describes a mouse caught in a glue trap in her house and the ethical dilemmas we face when it comes to caring for creation but also keeping pests out of our homes. Have you ever faced a dilemma of this kind? What did you do?

- Change is difficult, and yet it is an essential part of both this life and our transition to the one to come. In 1 Corinthians, the apostle Paul writes, "We will all be changed—in a flash, in the twinkling of an eye, at the last trumpet. For the trumpet will sound, the dead will be raised imperishable, and *we will be changed*." What do you think this final transformation will be like?

An invitation to action: Watch a video of fledgling birds and their parents online. What do you notice about how the parents care for them? What might this illustrate about how God cares for you in times of transition?

5. NOTICING

- Courtney visits the Cape May Birding Festival and discovers there are many additional ways to identify birds. She writes, "We can begin to learn how to see things we didn't even know to look for when someone helps us to open our eyes." Have you ever had an eye-opening experience? What was it like?

- Noticing the natural world can bring us great joy and comfort, but equally important is learning to notice what is happening inside of us when we experience change. How comfortable are you at asking yourself gentle, curious questions during times of stress? Do you have any favorites?

- Courtney writes that the Psalms "offer us a masterclass" when it comes to noticing and attending to our own feelings. Do you have a favorite psalm? What is it that draws you to it?

- Courtney is surprised when she sees Margaret Renkl's backyard on a news special. After reading Renkl's beautiful writing about it, she expects it to be studded with fairy dust of some kind, but in reality, it's just a yard. Yet Renkl has learned how to *see*. Are you adept at finding the miraculous in the mundane, or is your yard just a yard? How might you train your eyes to see more mystery and magic?

An invitation to action: Take a fifteen-minute awe walk this week. Commemorate it with a selfie.

6. ECOTONES

- Ecotones are transitional spaces where one or more habitats overlap. Have you ever visited an ecotone? What did you notice there?

- Courtney writes that ecotones are often very fruitful spaces, but also potentially dangerous ones. Have you experienced any particularly fruitful or dangerous transitions in your life? Share the story.

- Many animals (including humans!) learn through play. Practicing playful curiosity can help lead us through change with more openness and willingness. Can you think of a time when play helped you to process or assimilate a difficult change?

- Hebrews 11 chronicles many of our heroes of the faith—men and women who courageously followed God during difficult transitions. Put yourself in Noah's shoes for a moment. What would it feel like if God asked you to build a giant boat under a cloudless sky? How do you think Noah managed to trust God during this in-between time?

An invitation to action: Visit a community that is very different from yours this week. Attend a worship service in a different language than your primary one; visit an assisted living facility for games or conversation; volunteer to read books at an elementary school. What do you notice about your own heart in encountering difference? What did you learn about others? About yourself?

7. AGING

- Have you ever spotted a bird's nest? Where was it? Did you figure out what kind of birds used it?

- Courtney writes of Saul's exciting conversion in the book of Acts and her own, slower warming to the things of God. Tell (or write) your own come-to-Jesus story, if you have one. What stands out to you most about it?

- Where would you classify yourself in the aging process? Young? Middle-aged? On the older side? What has been the hardest part of aging for you so far?

- In what ways have you witnessed God's kindness to you during the aging process? What special grace does it have for you?

An invitation to action: Make a list of each of the difficult parts of aging you have faced (or are facing). Pray through it, asking for God's wisdom and mercy for each one.

8. FLOCKING

- How many different types of ducks were you familiar with before reading this chapter? Were you surprised by the number and diversity of ducks there are?

- For Courtney, ducks are a picture of a healthy congregation— diversity and difference, but everyone traveling in the same direction. Have you ever been part of a church like this? What was it like?

- Courtney describes changes her church made to accommodate her gluten intolerance, and the ways God calls us to bear with one another in love. Have you ever needed a special accommodation from a worshiping community? Were you accommodated without asking, or did you have to inquire? What was that process like?

- Courtney writes, "Going it alone is in my DNA." Yet she seeks to learn from the ducks that flock together, and has integrated practices into her ministry to make sure she connects more regularly with people. Are you naturally introverted or extroverted? How can you follow Bonhoeffer's instruction to lean into the goodness of both community and solitude?

An invitation to action: Find some ducks this week. Observe them. What do you notice about how they treat one another?

9. MIGRATION

- Did you know that most birds migrate in the dead of night? If your answer is yes, where did you first learn this information? If your answer is no, did it surprise you?

- Courtney writes of the German word *Zugunruhe,* or migration restlessness, writing that restlessness itself can be a clue that we may need a change. Have you ever felt this type of restlessness? What did you do about it?

- Discernment is the spiritual practice of seeking God, listening to wise counsel, and paying attention to our own hearts before we make a decision. Have you ever been in a season of discernment? How did it feel?

- Frederick Buechner writes of knowing that "all is right deep down" when we come to a right decision with God. Have you ever experienced this type of peace?

An invitation to action: Make a list of the wise people in your life who you would go to for counsel before a big decision. Save this list somewhere handy for the next time you need it.

10. URBAN WILDLIFE

- Do you have an urban wildlife story of your own? Share (or write) about it.

- In the book of Acts, Peter learns to adapt to the new reality of a church that welcomes both Jews and Gentiles. Met with a vision from God, he learns not to call unclean what God calls clean. After his vision he shares the gospel with Cornelius, a Roman soldier, and his friends and family. Have you ever needed to adapt your faith to a new and unexpected reality? What was it, and what did you do?

- Courtney shares the story of birds making nests out of anti-bird spikes—the very things meant to keep them from resting on buildings at all! What can we learn from the adaptability of these magpies about making our home in a sometimes hostile world?

- Courtney writes of the new creation, that she thinks it will be "more familiar than our next breath even while knocking us flat with its unexpected beauties." What do you think about when you ponder the new heaven and the new earth described in Revelation 21–22?

An invitation to action: Go scouting for urban (or suburban) wildlife this week. What birds and animals do you notice around your home, school, or office? What do you notice about their adaptability to human-centric spaces?

11. CLIMATE

- On a scale of 1 to 10, how often do you think about climate change? On the same scale, how much does it worry you? Why?

- Courtney writes of moral injury, the pain in knowing something didn't have to be this way. Have you ever experienced moral injury in your life? What triggered it, and what was your experience of it?

- C. S. Lewis wrote that our job, in the face of danger, was first "to pull ourselves together" and then, essentially, to keep doing all of the good and ordinary things of life. Courtney writes that this itself is a kind of resistance and testimony, that in the face of despair we would keep looking up. What ordinary things help tether you to the love of God during times of stress?

- Courtney quotes Psalm 12:1-2: *Help, Lord, for no one is faithful anymore.* Despair can drive us to isolation. Yet we are not alone. God calls us to be stewards of the earth, and many, many faith-based organizations are working to care well for creation. Who can you think of in your life that could be a conversation partner or a friend to you in your concern for the earth?

An invitation to action: Research local environmental policies in your area. Are there any you disagree with or would like to help make better? Look up your senator or congressperson and write a letter saying so today.

12. WINTER

- Do you have any favorite childhood memories of winter? Share one (or two!).

- Courtney likens winter to seasons of difficulty and unexpected change in our lives. She shares the story of her husband's rejection from a PhD program and how this devastating news affected them in the moment. What is one unexpected change you've faced in your life?

- Later on in the chapter, Courtney acknowledges that her husband's rejection from his PhD program actually served to shape their lives in a really fruitful and positive direction. Have you ever experienced a difficult change that felt brutal at the time but later proved good?

- In Luke 2, we meet Anna and Simeon, two faithful people who have been waiting at the temple for the Messiah. Anna in particular has suffered—widowed early, she has spent decades alone. Yet both Anna and Simeon receive the great honor of meeting the infant Jesus. Has a long season of winter (or suffering) ever borne good fruit in your life?

An invitation to action: If you are in a season of winter (hardship, suffering) today, spend some time in prayer, telling God of your struggle. If you are not, think back on a winter time in your life and give God thanks for seeing you through it.

13. MOLTING

- Have you ever seen a bird in molt? What did it look like?
- "Molting," Courtney writes, "is not a dignified process." This can be true of many types of physical change. Are there any difficult physical challenges you face today? Share the story, if you're comfortable.
- Courtney was particularly frustrated when a pastor's wife offered to "pray that" ailment out of her. Have you ever had an affliction minimized by someone? How did it feel? How did you respond in the moment? How do you *wish* you would have responded?
- Physical changes can make us feel exiled from our own bodies, confused about what lies ahead. In Jeremiah 29, the prophet tells God's people in exile to "seek the peace and prosperity of the city" to which he has brought them, even though it is not their home. Are there any ways God has helped you learn to seek peace in your body, even if all is not as healthy or strong as you'd wish?

An invitation to action: Take time this week to care for and thank your body for all it does for you. If you are ill or injured, give the parts of your body that have been suffering particularly tender care. Tell Jesus about your frustrations with your body—aging or ailments—and thank him for the parts that bring you joy.

14. WATER

- Have you ever stopped to think about water? What amazes you about it?

- Courtney describes how lakes turn over in winter, forming ice at the top rather than the bottom, and likens it to great disorder events in our lives that turn everything we knew on its head. She shares the story of her friend Sam, who died in a kayaking accident, as a disorder event of this kind. Have you ever experienced an event that turned everything you thought you knew upside down? Share (or write) the story.

- Courtney writes that she wants to be like the water that flexes rather than forces, flowing around obstacles rather than bulldozing them. Can you think of an example where you've been flexible like this? What happened?

- In 2 Kings, Elijah heads out into the wilderness despondent and afraid. He falls asleep under a scrubby bush, and an angel wakes him with food, water, and a message of rest. Have you ever been pushed to your limits? What happened when you reached them?

An invitation to action: Follow Elijah's lead and take a nap. A really *good* nap. Actually get in bed, close the curtains, put in your mouthguard (if you, like Courtney, sleep with one of those things), and let yourself rest deeply.

15. WIND

- How does it feel to know that tiny microbes are swirling around your head right at this very moment?

- When is it wise to ride the currents life sends us, and when should we try to steer the ship? How do you go about making these decisions in your life?

- Would you ever want to visit the Drake Passage? Why or why not?

- Wind is often a metaphor in Scripture for the Holy Spirit. In Acts, the Spirit shows up as a rushing wind, and later atop the disciples' heads like tongues of flame. Yet, Courtney writes, the Holy Spirit does not come to destroy but to draw together. Each of the disciples is given the power of translation, sharing the gospel in languages their listeners can understand. Many in the crowds respond with awe and faith, but others with cynicism, saying, "They have had too much wine." When you encounter the miraculous or the beautiful, are you more tempted toward praise or sarcasm? Why do you think this is?

An invitation to action: Look at the weather forecast and find the windiest day this week. Then, go outside to a spot you know will catch lots of wind (big, open fields are great for this, as are hilltops and beaches). Stand in one spot and play with the wind. What do you hear? Feel? What happens if you crouch down or extend your arms? Why do you think Scripture so often uses the metaphor of wind to describe the Holy Spirit?

16. PRAIRIE

- Have you ever lived near a prairie or visited one? What did you notice about it?

- Courtney writes of the pain of saying goodbye to her beloved Wisconsin congregation, but also of her friend Dale's perspective that nature, particularly prairie, "needs to be disturbed" in order to be healthy. Have there been any times in your life that change, even hard change, ushered in greater health (either for you physically or for your family or community)?

- "But of course," writes Courtney, "nature can be stressed too far." Have you ever experienced a change that pushed you beyond what you could handle? Share the story, if you're comfortable.

- In Joshua 2, we meet Rahab. She saves the Israelite spies sent to scout out her city of Jericho and in return, they save her. Rahab's name shows up in Matthew's genealogy of Jesus, a high honor for a woman who had a very rocky start. Courtney writes, "God-given change can set us on better paths, those we could never have discovered on our own." Have you ever experienced this sort of God-given change? What was its result?

An invitation to action: Look up your nearest prairie. Go visit it.

17. DECOMPOSITION

- When is the most recent time you've encountered decomposition? What is your general reaction to it?
- In what ways is decomposition an essential part of the natural world?
- Change transforms us. How has God been faithful to you in this beautiful, painful process?
- "Decomposition is a wonder," the nature guide tells Courtney after a soil-exploration exercise. Courtney writes that she finds hope in the knowledge that the story of God "precedes us and it will go on long after us, too. . . . So even in the breakdown of death, there is a bright, fine filament of hope." Where have you experienced hope, even in the face of death?

An invitation to action: Go outside. Find something dead. Study it. What do you see? Feel? Smell? In what ways is the death, even now, inviting new life?

18. ENDINGS

- Can you think of a recent ending in your life? What ended, and how did it feel?
- Courtney shares the story of Pongo, the pigeon that made a home in her backyard for six months. One day, Pongo disappeared without a trace. Have you ever experienced an unclear

ending like this in your life? Did the lack of certainty make things easier or more difficult?

- In Luke 12:22–32, Jesus tells us to consider the ravens and the wild flowers, reminders of God's concern and care for us. How might meditating on these words help you trust God with your own life? With your death?

- What is the most difficult part of accepting the change of endings for you? What ending do you most look forward to? Dread?

An invitation to action: Grab some art supplies (even a pencil and paper will do!). Read Revelation 1:1–5 and depict it artistically. What do you imagine this ending will be like?

CONCLUSION: WONDER

- When and where do you most often experience wonder?

- Courtney describes wonders she's encountered in the natural world, but also one particular act of generosity that floored her. In what ways can people drive us to wonder? Have you ever experienced a surprising act of generosity?

- In Mark 8:18, Jesus asks his disciples why they are failing to see and hear what he is really saying. Do you ever feel like you are missing what God intends for you to see or hear? How might you cultivate greater awareness of and sensitivity to the leading of God?

- How can wonder be a balm to us during times of difficult change? How can it help us build resilience?

An invitation to action: Think of an impending change in your life, big or small. Then, take it outside and walk or hike out your prayers surrounding it. If getting outdoors is tricky, sit near a window while you pray.

Notes

1. TOUGH TRANSITIONS

5   *I am not ready:* Margaret Renkl, *The Comfort of Crows* (Spiegel & Grau, 2023), 37.

   If we can let go: Brad Stulberg, *Master of Change: How to Excel When Everything Is Changing, Including You* (HarperOne, 2023), 27.

   The compassion Jesus offers: Henri Nouwen et al., *Compassion: A Reflection on the Christian Life* (Image, 2006), 18.

6   *The animals are more ancient:* John O'Donohue, *Anam Cara* (Harper Perennial, 1998), 53.

7   *Nature asks:* J. Drew Lanham, *Sparrow Envy: Field Guide to Birds and Lesser Beasts* (Hub City Press, 2021), 67.

2. STASIS

12   *Every branch:* John 15:2 NIV.

14   *Stillness is:* Paul Kingsnorth, *Savage Gods* (Two Dollar Radio, 2019), 39.

15   *A deeper magic:* C. S. Lewis, *The Lion, the Witch, and the Wardrobe* (HarperCollins, 1994).

17   *Lying in wait:* Lin-Manuel Miranda, *Hamilton: The Musical*, 2015.

3. FORESTS

25   *It is a curious circumstance:* Aldo Leopold, *A Sand County Almanac* (Oxford University Press, 2020), 79.

4. FLEDGING

29   *To be conscious:* Christian Wiman, *Zero at the Bone* (Farrar, Straus and Giroux, 2023), 29.

32   *Listen, I tell you a mystery:* 1 Corinthians 15: 51-52.

33   *Those who find their lives:* Matthew 16:25; 5:4; 20:16.

34   *Something that fundamentally shifts:* Brad Stulberg, *Master of Change: How to Excel When Everything Is Changing, Including You* (HarperOne, 2023), 2.

Change and disorder are the exceptions: Stulberg, *Master of Change,* 2.

5. NOTICING

42   *Nothing on earth:* Annie Dillard, *The Writing Life* (HarperPerennial, 1990), 98.

43   *I cannot carry:* Numbers 11:14-15 NIV.

My soul is downcast: Psalm 42:6, 9 NIV.

44   *Let me know thee:* Augustine, *Confessions,* Book X, trans. F. J. Sheed (Hackett, 1992), 173.

45   *One of the key features:* Nicholas Weiler, "'Awe Walks' Boost Emotional Well-Being," University of California San Francisco, September 21, 2020, www.ucsf.edu/news/2020/09/418551/awe-walks-boost-emotional-well -being.

46   *I think we almost:* Margaret Renkl, "41: Margaret Renkl and *The Comfort of Crows*," *The Thing with Feathers Podcast,* October 23, 2023, https://podcasts .apple.com/us/podcast/41-margaret-renkl-on-the-comfort-of-crows /id1666413692?i=1000632247843.

47   *Absolutely unmixed attention:* Simone Weil, *Gravity and Grace* (Bison Books, 1997), 170.

This is my son: Luke 9:32, 35 NIV.

6. ECOTONES

54   *The human journey:* John O'Donohue, *Anam Cara* (Harper Perennial, 1998), xvii.

55   *"Behold, I am":* Matthew 28:20 NIV.

7. AGING

58   *Wasting away:* 2 Corinthians 4:16 NIV.

relentless defoliation: Hannah Arendt, personal letter to Mary McCarthy, December 1974, in Blanche Wiesen Cook's "Hannah and Her Soul Sister: Two Players in the Cultural and Political Wars of Mid-century America," *Los Angeles Times,* March 12, 1995, www.latimes.com/archives/la-xpm -1995-03-12-bk-41586-story.html.

59 *Avoid storms:* David Wright, "Lines on Retirement after Reading Lear," Poets.org, https://poets.org/poem/lines-retirement-after-reading-lear. Used by permission of the author.

Like a tree planted: Psalm 1:3 NIV.

60 *She is clothed:* Proverbs 31:25.

61 *In the end:* Wright, "Lines on Retirement after Reading Lear."

Will last forever: Isaiah 51:6 NIV.

63 *Our perceptions are shaped:* Kenn Kaufman, *The Birds That Audubon Missed: Discovery and Desire in the American Wilderness* (Avid Reader Press, 2024), 326.

65 *Instead, you ought:* James 4:14-15 NIV.

The search to know: Peter Harris, *Under the Bright Wings* (Regent College Publishing, 2000), 12.

8. FLOCKING

69 *The person who loves:* Dietrich Bonhoeffer, *Life Together* (Augsburg Fortress, 1996), 36.

70 *Some ants have an extraordinary:* Tatiana Giraud et al., "Evolution of Supercolonies: The Argentine Ants of Southern Europe," *Proc Natl Acad Sci USA*, April 16, 2002, 6075-6079, www.pnas.org/doi/10.1073/pnas.09269 4199.

During territorial combat: Alice Laciny, et al., "Colobopsis explodens," ZooKeys, April 19, 2018, https://zookeys.pensoft.net/articles.php?id= 22661.

9. MIGRATION

75 *They will go unnoticed:* Kenn Kaufman, *The Birds That Audubon Missed: Discovery and Desire in the American Wilderness* (Avid Reader Press, 2024), 86.

80 *Their migratory pod:* See, for example, *Blue Planet II*, episode one, and "Mobula Rays Leap Through the Air: The Secret Life of Animals" from National Geographic.

Because I know who holds: Gloria Gaither and William J. Gaither, "Because He Lives," 1969.

82 *God has not abdicated:* Lore Ferguson Wilbert, *The Understory: An Invitation to Rootedness and Resilience from the Forest Floor* (Brazos Press, 2024), 125.

   All is right: Frederick Buechner, *Listening to Your Life* (HarperOne, 1992), 179-80.

10. URBAN WILDLIFE

86 *The urban monster:* Lyanda Lynn Haupt, *The Urban Bestiary: Encountering the Everyday Wild* (Little, Brown and Company, 2013), 91.

   You will receive power: Acts 1:8 NIV.

90 *They're outsmarting us:* Emily Anthes, "They're Outsmarting Us," *The New York Times,* July 13, 2023, www.nytimes.com/2023/07/13/science/magpies-birds-nests.html.

11. CLIMATE

94 *Humans are causing climate change:* "Do scientists agree on climate change?" NASA, https://science.nasa.gov/climate-change/faq/do-scientists-agree-on-climate-change/.

95 *Why, Lord, do you stand:* Psalm 10:1 NIV.

96 *In a world racked:* Kyle Meyaard-Schaap, *Following Jesus in a Warming World: A Christian Call to Climate Action* (InterVarsity Press, 2023), 72.

   Learn to do right: Isaiah 1:17 NIV.

97 *Action on behalf of life:* Robin Wall Kimmerer, *Braiding Sweetgrass* (Milkweed Editions, 2013), 340.

98 *As long as it is day:* John 9:4 NIV.

   You think your pain: Jane Howard, "Telling Talk from a Negro Writer," *Life Magazine,* May 24, 1963.

   Common curse: Makoto Fujimura, X, November 15, 2024, https://x.com/iamfujimura/status/1857622089034809483.

99 *If we are all going to be destroyed:* C. S. Lewis, "On Living in an Atomic Age," *Present Concerns: Essays by C. S. Lewis,* 73–74; *Living in an Atomic Age* by CS Lewis © copyright 1948 CS Lewis Pte Ltd. Extract used with permission.

102 *A man of sorrows:* Isaiah 53:3 NKJV.

   Only if we face: James Baldwin, "Telling Talk from a Negro Writer," *LIFE Magazine,* May 24, 1963.

12. WINTER

106   *Plants and animals don't fight:* Katherine May, *Wintering: The Power of Rest and Retreat in Difficult Times* (Riverhead, 2020), 14.

The forces shaping life: Peter J. Marchand, *Life in the Cold: An Introduction to Winter Ecology* (University Press of New England, 2014), 2.

108   *Think of only one thing:* "Barth Challenges Bonhoeffer to Return to Germany." *Preaching Today,* www.preachingtoday.com/illustrations/2003 /september/14570.html.

Granted, I did not refuse: Wyatt Houtz, "The Life of Karl Barth: Protesting in Germany 1930-1935," *PostBarthian,* June 8, 2018, https://postbarthian .com/2018/06/08/the-life-of-karl-barth-protesting-in-nazi-germany-1930 -1935-part-4/.

110   *Worshiped night and day:* Luke 2:37 NIV.

Sovereign Lord: Luke 2:29-30 NIV.

13. MOLTING

115   *Catherine of Siena:* "Saint Catherine of Siena," Franciscan Media, accessed July 15, 2025, www.franciscanmedia.org/saint-of-the-day/saint-catherine-of-siena/.

116   *I just sat out on my deck:* Courtney Ellis, "14: Practicing Curiosity, Birds of Saskatchewan, + Mary the Blue Jay (microbiologist Dr. Janet Hill)," *The Thing With Feathers Podcast,* April 14, 2023, https://podcasts.apple.com/us /podcast/14-practicing-curiosity-birds-of-saskatchewan-mary/id1666413 692?i=1000609252651.

117   *Most birds:* Courtney Ellis, "64: What Birds are the Most Metal? (Dan Baldassarre)," *The Thing With Feathers Podcast,* April 15, 2024, https://podcasts .apple.com/us/podcast/64-what-birds-are-the-most-metal-dan-baldas sarre/id1666413692?i=1000652462268.

118   *Is also ordered:* Ted Floyd, *How to Know the Birds* (National Geographic, 2019), 183.

119   *Seek the peace:* Jeremiah 29:7 NIV.

14. WATER

121   *The mixing of surface:* Peter J. Marchand, *Life in the Cold* (University Press of New England, 2014), 135.

124   *Water does not resist:* Margaret Atwood, *The Penelopiad* (Canongate Books, 2018), 43.

131   *This far you may come:* Job 38:11 NIV.

"I have had enough": 1 Kings 19:4 NIV.

15. WIND

138　*All we know:* Barbara Mahany, *The Book of Nature: The Astonishing Beauty of God's First Sacred Text* (Broadleaf Books, 2023), 93.

139　*When air from a region:* Luis Garcia, "Weather Wednesday: Santa Ana Winds," National Weather Service, December 11, 2024, www.kget.com /weather/weather-wednesdays/weather-wednesday-santa-ana-winds.

140　*The wind blows wherever:* John 3:8 NIV.

144　*The bridge would be lighter:* "Golden Gate Bridge: Leon Moisseiff," PBS, accessed March 16, 2025, www.pbs.org/wgbh/americanexperience/features /goldengate-moisseiff/.

145　*No discipline seems pleasant:* Hebrews 12:11 NIV.

16. PRAIRIE

148　*Consider it pure joy:* James 1:2-4 NIV.

149　*A flourishing Christian faith:* Karen Swallow Prior, "Christian Nationalism's Failure of Imagination," *The Dispatch,* June 23, 2024, https://thedispatch .com/newsletter/dispatch-faith/karen-swallow-prior-christian-nation alisms-failure-of-imagination/.

　　　75 to 80 percent of the biomass: Tallgrass Prairie National Preserve, Kansas, "A Complex Prairie Ecosystem," National Park Service, https://home.nps .gov/tapr/learn/nature/a-complex-prairie-ecosystem.htm.

　　　It was like digging: Aldo Leopold, *A Sand County Almanac* (Oxford University Press, 2020), 46.

150　*For a few years:* Aldo Leopold, *A Sand County Almanac,* 43.

　　　Why you should stop complimenting: Keisha "TK" Dutes et al., "Why You Should Stop Complimenting People for Being Resilient," *Life Kit on NPR,* August 25, 2022, www.npr.org/2022/08/16/1117725653/why-being-resilient -might-matter-less-than-you-think.

　　　I swear if I get called: Carly Berlin and Halle Parker, "If I Get Called 'Resilient' One More Time . . . ," *Sea Change,* May 23, 2023, www.wwno.org /podcast/sea-change/2023-05-23/if-i-get-called-resilient-one-more-time.

152　*I pray that as you trust:* Ephesians 3:17 First Nations Version.

153　*The greatest bird decline:* Rebecca Heiseman, "Prairie Plight: Five of the Fastest Declining Grassland Birds in the U.S.," *American Bird Conservancy,* January 7, 2025, https://abcbirds.org/blog/declining-grassland-birds.

17. DECOMPOSITION

157   *Anyone who loves:* John 12:24-25 NIV.

     Do not hold: John 20:17 NIV.

160   *Burying was iffy:* Edwin Rios, "The First Viral Video Ever Was Recorded 45 Years Ago Today," *Mother Jones*, November 15, 2013, www.motherjones .com/politics/2015/11/first-viral-video-ever-was-recorded-45-years-ago -today.

161   *We do not grow:* Lore Ferguson Wilbert, *The Understory: An Invitation to Rootedness and Resilience from the Forest Floor* (Brazos Press, 2024), 200.

162   *The dark night of the soul:* Christian Wiman, *Zero at the Bone* (Farrar, Straus and Giroux, 2023), 57.

     The old song of my spirit: Howard Thurman, *The Mood of Christmas* (Friends United Press, 2011), 158.

164   *Soil is the great connector:* Wendell Berry, *The Unsettling of America* (Counterpoint, 2004), 86.

165   *Even the limited awareness:* Peter Harris, *Under the Bright Wings* (Regent University Press, 2000), 35.

     To see beauty: Debbie Blue, *Consider the Birds: A Provocative Guide to Birds of the Bible* (Abingdon Press, 2013), 80.

18. ENDINGS

169   *You are a mist:* James 4:14 NIV.

     All people are like grass: 1 Peter 1:24 NIV.

170   *Strong bonds with parents:* Duane Bidwell, *After the Worst Day Ever: What Sick Kids Know About Sustaining Hope in Chronic Illness* (Beacon Press, 2024), 50.

     Children's stories of hope: Bidwell, *After the Worst Day Ever*, 143.

171   *Consider how the wild flowers grow:* Luke 12:27 NIV.

     Each day will have enough trouble: Matthew 6:34 NIV.

174   *Peace is the active rest:* Paul J. Pastor, *The Listening Day: Meditation on the Way,* Volume Two (Zeal Books, 2017), 25.

     They enjoy a seamless presence: John O'Donohue, *Anam Cara* (Harper Perennial, 2022), 53.

     There will be no more death: Revelation 21:4 NIV.

CONCLUSION

175   *He was not afraid:* J. A. Baker, *The Peregrine* (NYRB Classics, 2004), 162.

[Baker] wrote The Peregrine: Robert Macfarlane, introduction to *The Peregrine* (NYRB Classics, 2004), ix-x.

176   *Do you have eyes:* Mark 8:18 NIV.

Not poor like sweet church mice: Kate Bowler, *Everything Happens for a Reason: And Other Lies I've Loved* (Random House, 2018), 38.

178   *Beauty is its own excuse:* Kent Gramm, *Nature's Bible: The Old Testament through the Eyes of Creation* (Resource Publications, 2023), 5.

179   *Adopt the pace:* Ralph Waldo Emerson, *Nature* (James Munroe and Company, 1836).

The land knows you: Robin Wall Kimmerer, *Braiding Sweetgrass* (Milkweed Editions, 2015), 36.

181   *What is to give light:* Anton Wildgans, "Helldunkle Stunde," Poemist, www .poemist.com/anton-wildgans/helldunkle-stunde#google_vignette, translated from the German with help from my husband, Daryl Ellis.

183   *Joy is at the end:* Frederick Buechner, *Listening to Your Life* (HarperOne, 1992), 272.